SHIPWRECKS
Disasters of the Deep Seas

Nigel Cawthorne

ARCTURUS

Contents

Arcturus Publishing Limited
26/27 Bickels Yard
151–153 Bermondsey Street
London SE1 3HA

Published in association with
foulsham
W. Foulsham & Co. Ltd,
The Publishing House, Bennetts Close, Cippenham,
Slough, Berkshire SL1 5AP, England

ISBN 0-572-03145-9

This edition printed in 2005

Copyright © 2005, Arcturus Publishing Limited

British Library Cataloguing-in-Publication Data: a catalogue record for
this book is available from the British Library

Printed in China

Cover images:
Front, 'The Wreck of the *Titanic*', oil painting by Stuart
Williamson; back flap, Human remains on a Japanese
shipwreck in Truk Lagoon, Truk Islands, photograph by
Hal Beral/CORBIS

Cover Design by Steve Flight and Beatriz Waller
Design by Steve Flight
Layout by Steve West

Introduction

From the time of the Phoenicians until the birth of the jet-plane, ships were the principal means of transporting people or goods over long distances. Travel by sea, though, was beset by dangers. Taking to the oceans, humankind put itself at the mercy of the great forces of nature. Ships have been overwhelmed by huge waves, consumed by fire, sunk by storms and driven onto uncharted rocks to break apart. They have collided with icebergs or other ships, or run aground on unlit coastlines at night. Boilers have exploded. Magazines have ignited. Cargoes have shifted with catastrophic consequences and submarines have submerged never to come up again.

Not all sinkings have been accidental. Pirates happily scuttled their prey with all souls. Wreckers used lanterns on cliff tops to mimic the lights of a local harbour and lure hapless ships onto the rocks. Even those who made it ashore alive were not safe. If just one of those aboard escaped with his life, the wreck was not open for plunder: Daniel Defoe wrote of 'poor distressed seamen when they come on shore by force of a tempest, and seek help for their lives, and where they find the rocks themselves not more merciless than the people who range about them for their prey'.

War also produced its historic wrecks. A German submarine torpedoed the *Lusitania* in 1915, radically altering America's attitude to World War I and eventually bringing the United States into the war on the Allied side. The wreck of the USS *Arizona*, sunk during the attack on Pearl Harbor in 1941, is now an American national memorial. The worst shipwreck in history occurred in January 1945 when the *Wilhelm Gustloff*, packed with refugees, was sunk by a Russian submarine off Danzig, killing over 9,000 people.

Though most long-distance travellers now prefer to travel by air, there are still shipping accidents that result in a shocking loss of life. In September 2002, the Senagalese ferry *Joola* capsized and sank off the coast of Gambia, killing more than 1,800, and in December 1987, in an accident regarded as the worst peacetime tragedy at sea, the Philippine ferry, the *Dona Paz*, collided with the tanker *Vector*, drowning over 4,300.

Oil tankers aground – and the terrible environmental consequences – also make the headlines. The clean-up after the sinking of the *Exxon Valdez* cost the company over $2 billion, with a further $1 billion spent on contingent court cases.

The lure of sunken treasure ships has divers searching the sea bottom. In 1985, retired chicken farmer Mel Fisher brought up an estimated $50 million worth of goods from a wreck off the Florida Keys. He had found the legendary *Nuestra Señora de Atocha*, the most richly laden galleon ever to leave the New World, which went down in 1622. Meanwhile, the latest submersibles are used to search out the watery graves of the *Titanic* and the *Bismarck*, while great care is taken in raising

historic wrecks such as *The Flagship of Henry VIII*, and the *Mary Rose*.

Shipwrecks have a unique power over the imagination. They are the stuff of great literature, featuring in *Robinson Crusoe*, *Gulliver's Travels*, *The Tempest* and *Twelfth Night*. At least seven movies and countless TV shows have been made about the sinking of the *Titanic*. Currently, there are 1,189 items on the catalogue of the British Library about shipwrecks. It is a subject of enduring interest.

No book on maritime disasters can be comprehensive – in the 1860s alone 2,537 British ships sank in deep water according to Lloyd's of London – *Shipwrecks* selects the sinkings with the greatest loss of life, the most famous vessels, the richest treasure troves, the most archaeologically significant wreck sites and the most daring rescues. It tells the tales of the fate of the victims, the disastrous mistakes made by ships' captains and navigators, the impossible conditions faced at sea, the courage of those who survived and the audacious attempts, some successful, others not, to raise what now lies at the bottom of the sea.

Athenian trireme from the time of the Battle of Salamis, 480BC

1 Wooden Warships

Warships are built to sink and be sunk, so it is not surprising that the seabed is littered with their wrecks.

The earliest known war at sea took place in 1231BC, when the Egyptians took on what they called the 'Sea Peoples' – a disparate group of peoples from Greece, Anatolia, Crete and Sicily. They were eventually defeated by Ramses III, ruler of Egypt from 1198BC to 1166BC. Nothing has been found of warships of that era. Indeed, the only evidence of shipwrecks from prehistory has come from merchant ships, rather than warships, because, although the ships' timbers rotted away, the ceramic amphorae which carried the ships' cargo did not.

The Greeks, however, developed triremes, light, oar-powered warships designed to ram enemy vessels. In 1980, the bronze ram of one of these fighting ships was discovered in the sea 650 feet offshore at Athlit, south of Haifa in Israel. Nothing was left of the ship that carried the Athlit ram. It seems to have been wrecked when it came in too close to shore and has since disintegrated, leaving only the ram, which is seven feet long, two-and-a-half feet wide and weighs over a thousand pounds. Sixteen of the ship's timbers would have fitted inside the ram. These heavy timbers would have effectively made the whole of the bottom of the ship a weapon: at any sort of speed,

it would have carried huge momentum which would have driven the ram home.

The ram itself was made from high-grade bronze: 10 per cent iron and 90 per cent copper. Jutting out from the bow at the water line, its tip ended in three narrow fins that spread the impact out over an area approximately one-and-a-half feet square. The idea was not to penetrate the hull of the enemy ship, as the ram might get stuck. Rather, the aim was to smash the planks of the enemy ship, so that it would fill with water and sink.

Four symbols cast in the surface of the ram also appear on coins minted in Cyprus between 204BC and 164BC, suggesting the ram was probably manufactured in the port of Paphos on Cyprus and was carried on a ship in the fleet of the Macedonian kings of Egypt, Ptolemy V Epiphanes or his successor Ptolemy VI Philometor. The ship, it is thought, was a tetreres – that is, it had four tiers of oars as opposed to the trireme's three – but the circumstances of its loss remain a mystery.

The remains of two Carthaginian warships came to light off Marsala in Sicily in the early 1970s when the stern of one and the complete hull of another were found preserved under a sandbank. It is thought that the ships were making for the shelter of the port, at that time called Lilybaeum, after a sudden change in wind direction had given the Romans victory at the Battle of the Egadi Islands in 241BC, ending the First Punic War. The ships were new when they sank and they seem to have been built in haste, as carpenter's shavings were found on board.

The ships would each have been 115 feet long with a beam of just sixteen feet. They had two banks of fifteen oars, each pulled by two men, which would have made them very fast indeed. The bow carried a ram, but unlike the Athlit ram, this was a separate unit, held in place by long nails which would have snapped off if the ram became snagged.

Painted lettering on the hulls was in the Phoenician-Punic script and butcher-cut animal bones found on board revealed the meat-rich diet of the Carthaginians, and along with olives, nuts and other foodstuffs onboard, there were also quantities of marijuana. Green leaves were found imbedded in the putty and fragments of human and dog bones were found amongst the rock used as ballast, all of which provided a wealth of archaeological information.

Five small Roman galleys were found in 1981 near Mainz, Germany, perfectly preserved in the mud of the Rhine. These sleek, shallow-draught ships were used as patrol boats along the rivers of northern Europe. Built of oak, they date from the third and fourth century AD. No one knows in what circumstances they were sunk. The remains are now housed in the Museum of Ancient Shipping in Mainz.

Five Viking ships, including two warships, dating from around AD1000 were found in the mud of Skuldelev harbour in Denmark. The warships were of the type used to invade England around this time, and they appear to have been scuttled to block the harbour entrance. The larger

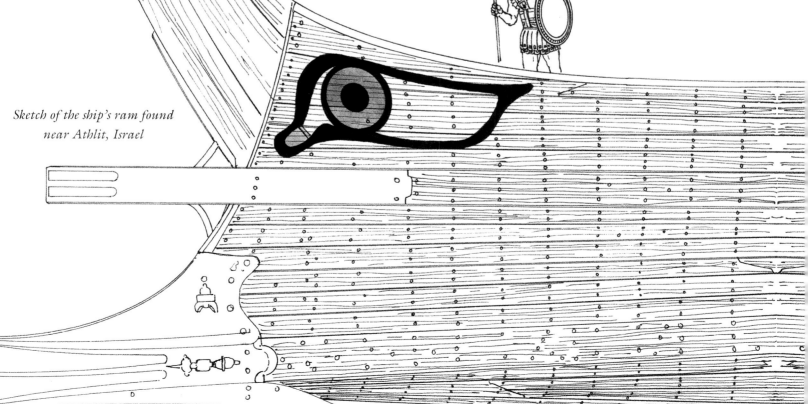

Sketch of the ship's ram found near Athlit, Israel

Viking longboat on display at the Viking Museum, Oslo, Norway

of the two was 120 feet long and big enough to carry cavalry. This type of boat was also used by the Vikings to reach Constantinople in 1043, and later by the Normans in their invasion of England in 1066.

The wreck of the *Grace Dieu*, a ship built for Henry V in 1417, was found in the River Hamble in 1859. A tall ship which would have towered over the other fighting ships of the day, she was built in response to French raids on the English coast. When her first voyage in 1420 ended in mutiny, however, the *Grace Dieu* was towed into the River Hamble where she was struck by lightning and burnt to the water line. The remains were gradually buried in mud, but can still be seen when they are exposed at low spring tides.

In 1962, the wreck of a Venetian fighting galley was found at the bottom of Lake Garda in northern Italy. Built in 1438, it had been transported there as part of a Venetian fleet during a war with the Duchy of Milan. Venice won and the fleet remained stationed at the east of the lake. In 1509, as Venice found itself under attack by France, the Holy Roman Emperor and the Pope, the Venetian admiral, Zaccaria Loredani, found himself heavily outnumbered and scuttled his ships. The galley was 130 feet long and had a broad platform on the front, known as a *rembata*, for carrying troops, along with mangonels – stone-throwing machines – and early cannon.

The first wreck of a ship with gun ports to be found was that of the Genoese warship *Lomellina*, which foundered off Villefranche-sur-Mer near Nice in a hurricane on 15 September 1516. She was under repair, and her capstan and other equipment had been dismantled when the hurricane struck. Under the driving force of the winds, the *Lomellina* heeled over and sank, settling on the bottom of the sea on her port side, where she still lies. There were wood chips and sawdust between the frames and a carpenter's plane was found nearby. Marine archaeologists examining the site have also found fifteen wrought-iron guns and their carriages, shot made of stone, iron and lead, and early hand grenades.

A caravel, once thought to be Columbus's *Pinta*, was found on Molasses Reef in the Turks and Caicos Islands in 1976. It is from the early sixteenth century and is the oldest extant wreck in the Americas. The ship was heavily armed and

A replica of the Santa Maria, *built as part of the 500th anniversary celebrations of Columbus's arrival in the Americas*

The Spanish Armada retreats in disarray from the English navy. Although few ships of the Armada were actually lost in battle, many were wrecked by storms and heavy seas as they attempted to sail home around Scotland and Ireland

carried leg irons, probably used for slaving: that part of the Caribbean was depopulated by Spanish slavers in that era. Disturbingly, some of the leg irons were locked, indicating that whoever was wearing them drowned. It is believed that most of the crew escaped from the ship before she sank, though from the artefacts remaining no one seems to have returned to salvage the wreck, indicating that the escaping crew might have been murdered by the natives. If they had survived, they would almost certainly have been marooned on the island for the rest of their lives. Intriguingly, among the ballast was black limestone which came from quarries near Bristol, along with rock from Lisbon and the mid-Atlantic islands.

Columbus did lose his flagship, the *Santa Maria*, on his first voyage to the Americas in 1492, the first recorded shipwreck in the New World. She ran aground on a shoal of reefs off Cap-Haïtien on the island of Hispaniola. When Columbus was unable to refloat her, he stripped her of her supplies and equipment, and used her timbers to build the colony of La Navidad, where thirty-nine of Columbus's men lived while the convoy returned to Spain. Three centuries later the anchor of the *Santa Maria* was found in Grande Riviere, Haiti. Then in 1949, the remains of a hull were spotted on the reef, though its exact location was not recorded. The wreck has not been rediscovered, but an anchor, grapeshot and iron bars of the type used as ballast on warships, along with other artefacts, have been found.

A wreck similar to the Molasses Reef wreck was found at Highborn Cay in the Bahamas which was also from the early sixteenth century and seems to have been at anchor when it sank. From the amount of armaments on board, it is thought to have been a pirate vessel.

The Remnants of the Armada

The Spanish Armada littered the seas around Britain with wrecks. Of the 130 ships that set out from Spain to invade England in 1588, only sixty returned home. But very few were lost in battle. After the English had succeeded in dispersing the Armada in the Channel, making invasion impossible, the Spaniards tried to sail around the north of the British Isles to return to Spain and found themselves driven onto the shores of Scotland and Ireland by a storm, which the English generally regarded as having divine origin.

The 800-ton *San Juan de Sicilia* was badly damaged in the fighting in the Channel, with one of her crew reporting that she had been hit by many shots from 'alow and aloft and from the prow to the stern, and below the water line in places difficult to repair'. Separated from the main body of the fleet on the way home, she limped into Tobermory Bay on Mull to make repairs. A few days later she exploded and sank, probably sabotaged. There were few survivors from the stricken vessel, apart from a shore party who escaped via Edinburgh to Flanders, at that time under Spanish control. A few years after the sinking of the *San Juan de Sicilia*, the rumour spread that there was treasure on board. The wreck was pillaged, but no treasure was ever found, although a bronze cannon that once belonged to the French king Francis I, now in Inveraray Castle, was thought to have been recovered around the time.

The flagship of the Armada's supply squadron, *El Gran Grifón*, was badly damaged during an encounter with Sir Francis Drake's *Revenge* and was sinking by the time she reached Fair Isle, between Orkney and the Shetland Islands. She drove aground in the narrow creek of Stroms Hellier at the southeast corner of the island on 27 September 1588 and the crew scrambled ashore. The wreck was found in 1970. Of her thirty-eight guns, eight had been newly cast in bronze. These cannon had been manufactured in some haste for the Armada, and their bores were so far off centre that these guns were not just useless but, for the operator, positively dangerous as well.

The *Girona* was one of four galleasses – ships with both oars and sails – to sail with the Armada. They came from Naples, another Spanish possession at that time. Displacing 600 tons and carrying fifty guns, the *Girona* had had her Mediterranean-style triangular lateen rig replaced in Lisbon with a square rig better suited to Atlantic sailing. She was the only one of the four galleasses unscathed by battle, but she was badly damaged by the subsequent storms and put into Killibegs on the west coast of Ireland to make repairs. There she was met by the survivors of two other Armada ships that had been wrecked on the coast. The 820-ton *Rata Encoronada* had foundered in Blacksod Bay, County Mayo, where the passengers and crew, which included the flower of the Spanish aristocracy, were led ashore by Don Alonso de Leiva, a favourite of Philip II. They boarded the *Duquesa Santa Ana* which was sheltering in nearby a cove. She promptly ran aground at Loughros Mor Bay, Donegal. Coming ashore, Don Alonso was injured and had to be carried on a litter to Killibegs. Once the repairs to the *Girona* were completed, she set off carrying the crews from all ships – 1,300 men in all – and tried to make for neutral Scotland. Her rudder broke off at the Giant's Causeway, Country Antrim, and she was driven onto Lacada Point. Only a handful of men survived. The tides and currents there have smashed the wreck to pieces, but a lot of gold and silver has been recovered, along with a thousand coins, Renaissance jewellery and knightly orders, including the insignia of the

There were few survivors from the stricken vessel, apart from a shore party who escaped via Edinburgh to Flanders

The English fleet under Lord Howard of Effingham and Sir Francis Drake engages the Armada off Cadiz

knights of Santiago, which almost certainly belonged to Don Alonso himself, and the cross of a knight of Malta, thought to have belonged to the *Girona's* captain, Fabricio Spinola.

The 945-ton *Santa Maria de la Rosa* was built in the Basque country as the mother ship for the Newfoundland whaling fleet, but was pressed into service with the Armada. Fitted with twenty-six guns, she carried the 225 men of the Sicilian infantry regiment (Sicily was also then under Spanish control). Storm-damaged before she even reached the Channel, she had to put into Corunna for a new mainmast. During the fighting, she was holed four times, once close to the water line. Separated from the main fleet on the homeward leg, she sought shelter from the gale in Basket Sound on the southwest tip of Ireland on 21 September 1588. The wind and tide drove her onto the reef in the middle of the sound where she sank, leaving only one survivor. The reef seems to have torn the bottom out of this ship, releasing the ballast, which has been found. Free of its ballast the rest of the ship appears to have slipped into deep water where it was lost. However, the muskets, arquebuses and other artefacts have been found, including two pieces of pewter stamped with the name Matute. The fleet muster rolls record that a Captain Francisco Ruiz Matute was the commander of the Sicilian infantry on board.

La Trinidad Valencera, a Venetian bulk-grain carrier, was also pressed into service with the Armada. Displacing 1,100 tons, she carried 281 men of a Neapolitan regiment under Don Alonso de Luzon. Among her forty-two guns were four siege guns with land carriages, which were intended to play a key role in the English campaign once the Armada had landed. Only lightly damaged in the fighting, *La Trinidad* became detached from the main fleet on the homeward voyage and began taking on water. She ran aground in Kinnegoe Bay on the north coast of Ireland on 14 September 1588. With the help of the locals, over the next two days, Don Alonso got most of his men ashore. Then on 16 September, the ship broke up, killing the Spaniards remaining on board and some Irishmen who were looting her. The survivors were rounded up by the English garrison. The officers were held for ransom, while the rest of the crew were massacred, though some escaped in the confusion and managed the perilous journey home via Scotland. Don Alonso and a handful of officers were eventually repatriated. The wreck was discovered in 1971 and identified by her siege guns. The wrecks of three more of *La Trinidad Valencera's* Levant squadron – the *Juliana*, the *Lavia* and the *Santa Maria de Vision* – were found together off Streedagh Strand, County Sligo, in 1986.

The discovery of *La Trinidad Valencera* helped explain how the 'invincible Armada' was so easily outgunned by the English. Guns and ammunition had been hastily assembled from all parts of the Spanish empire and there was no standardisation. In the heat of battle, Spanish gunners were having to measure shot to see whether it would fit the barrels of their guns. On *La Trinidad Valencera* a wooden 'gunner's rule' was found. This was used to calibrate shot. But when it was examined closely it proved to be so inaccurate that it was less than useless. Spanish survivors reckoned that the English could fire 2,000 rounds in the time the Spaniards could loose off just 750. English gunnery – and the British Atlantic coast – had proven too much for the Armada to handle.

The Spanish also lost warships in the Americas: in 1636, the *San Salvador* caught fire and exploded off Martinique, while the 850-ton, forty-two-gun *San Felipe*, bound from Spain to Cartagena, was wrecked with another ship off the island of Bonaire, in the Lesser Antilles, in 1610. Divers have recovered all the cannon from two of the three wrecks and much of the cargo from the *San Felipe*.

France and England at War

The French were also having trouble with their warships at the time. The wrecks of five first rate warships sunk off the coast of Normandy in 1692 show that they had been given a coating of resin along the water line which aimed to speed up slow, poor sailers. It did no good. They were caught by the English and burnt to the water line and now lie in twenty feet of water off Saint-Vaast-La-Hougue. Found in 1990, the wrecks have yielded some 350 artefacts which are now housed in the Maritime Museum on the small island of Tatihou.

By the middle of the eighteenth century, French warship design had improved immeasurably. In 1744, they launched the seventy-four-gun *L'Invincible*. Built in Rochefort, she had a revolutionary design that incorporated a great deal of iron to support the heavy gun decks. These supports were secured by huge nuts which would work loose with the vibration of the guns or in heavy seas and would have to be retightened. In action in 1745, *L'Invincible* fought off three English warships. But on 14 May 1747, at the first Battle of Cape Finisterre, off the Spanish coast, she was overwhelmed by a squadron of fourteen English ships under Admiral Lord Anson, a naval hero famed for plundering Spanish treasure ships off the coast of Chile and for being the first British naval officer to sail into Chinese waters. Captured, *L'Invincible* was sailed back to Portsmouth, where she was renamed HMS *Invincible* and became the pride of the British fleet. Her design was copied and 'seventy-fours' became the mainstay of the Royal Navy for the next one hundred years. At the beginning of the Seven Years' War (1756-63) she

Detail from 'The Blowing up of the French Commander's Ship
L'Orient *at the Battle of the Nile' by John Thomas Serres*

raided French possessions in Canada. Returning to North America in 1758 with a large squadron, she ran aground on a sandbank off Portsmouth on 19 February. Efforts were made to free her, but she was holed by her own anchor and sank. A salvage team managed to get her guns off, but the *Invincible* lay hidden under the waves until 1979, when a fisherman snagged his nets on her. The sands of the Solent had preserved a treasure trove of artefacts, including navigational instruments, rigging blocks, barrels of powder, bosun's stores and the square wooden platters the crew ate their meals from – giving us the expression 'square meal'. Another curiosity found on board was a large number of tompions. These were the wooden blocks used to plug the barrels of guns to keep the sea water out and from the number found, it has been deduced that the guns were

kept loaded at all times and sealed with a tompion.

In 1801, another seventy-four-gun HMS *Invincible* was wrecked on Harborough Sands off Yarmouth, killing four hundred. By this time the English and French were at war again. On 1 July 1798, the French Army had landed in Egypt to the west of Alexandria, as part of Napoleon's scheme to establish an empire in the Middle East and threaten the British position in India. His supply lines across the Mediterranean were protected by four frigates and fourteen ships of the line under Vice-Admiral François-Paul Brueys d'Aigalliers. On 1 August, Nelson with a fleet of eleven, caught them unawares sitting at Aboukir Bay. In the furious fighting that followed, Brueys' 120-gun flagship *L'Orient* blew up, killing the admiral and crew. The massive explosion so shocked both sides that there was a temporary cease-fire. But Nelson was not going to give away the advantage. Urging his men on, he sank three more French ships and captured nine. Nelson's victory at the Battle of the Nile made him a national hero and ended Napoleon's ambitions in the East.

In 1983 the wreck of *L'Orient* was found. On board there was Arabic printing type which Napoleon had taken from the Vatican print shop after his invasion of Italy, intending to use it to print his various proclamations. The ship's thirty-six-pound guns and her huge forty-six-foot copper-sheathed rudder were also found. A bronze plate on it bears the name *Dauphin Royal*, the original name of *L'Orient*. (After the French Revolution, her name had been changed to *Sans Culotte*, in honour of the revolutionaries, then to *L'Orient* as an acclamation of Napoleon's eastern ambitions.) Nearby, the wrecks of the forty-gun frigate *Artemise* and the frigate *Serieuse* have also been found. Wood from the shattered mast of *L'Orient* was used to make Nelson's coffin after he died at Trafalgar in 1805.

The wrecks of French and British warships are also to be found in the Americas. In August 1689, Sir William Phips sailed from Boston with 2,200 militiamen aboard thirty-four ships with the aim of ousting the French from Canada. Arriving at Quebec on 16 October, Phips demanded its surrender. The governor of New France, Louis de Buade, Comte de Palluau et de Frontenac, said that he would reply to Phips's demand *'par la bouche de mes canons'* – 'from the mouths of my cannon'. Phips bombarded the city and landed troops, but the French held out. By November winter was on its way and Phips was forced to lift the siege, losing four ships in the process. One of them, the *Elizabeth and Mary*, carrying a company of militiamen from Dorchester, Massachusetts, was lost without a trace. No one knew what had

In the furious battle that followed, Brueys' 120-gun flagship *L'Orient* blew up, killing the admiral and crew

happened to it until December 1994 when a local diver's mooring lines became tangled in some wreckage off L'Anse aux Bouleaux in the Gulf of St Lawrence. Over the next three years, the wreck was investigated and found to be that of the *Elizabeth and Mary*. Among the militiamen's muskets, pistols and bandoliers a pewter porringer was found. It had the initials 'M, S and I' on it. These were the initials of Sarah and Increase Mosley, who lived in Dorchester. Increase had been on Phips's ill-fated expedition and did not return. Sarah waited patiently for him for thirteen years before remarrying in 1703.

Fire was always a hazard for wooden ships. On the freezing night of 17 January 1744, HMS *Astrea* was at anchor in the harbour at Portsmouth, New Hampshire, when she caught fire. In an attempt to keep the ship warm, the stove had been over-stoked and the timbers beneath caught fire. A strong wind fanned the flames and spread the fire through the vessel. The crew set up a bucket chain, but the weather was so cold that the water in the buckets was frozen by the time it reached the flames. They abandoned ship and let her drift down the Piscatauqua River towards Goat Island, where the *Astrea* burnt to the water line and sank. There was no loss of life. In the nineteenth century, the pilings of a bridge were driven through what remained of the hulk, but divers have since salvaged numerous items from the wreck.

A second HMS *Astrea* was lost off the Virgin Islands on 23 May 1808. It was a clear night and the wind was freshening as a few minutes before eight o'clock gunner George Lovet came on watch. He was leaning on the port rail as his eyes became accustomed to the dark, when a line of breakers appeared dead ahead. At his cry, the captain turned hard to port, but it was too late. The *Astrea* struck the reef and began taking on water. The crew manned the pumps and an anchor line was laid in case it was possible to refloat her, but the wind and the waves were driving her onto the reef, and soon she was in danger of capsizing. The masts were cut away, and the frigate's thirty-two cannon were jettisoned in an effort to lighten her, but this only allowed the wind and waves to drive her further up the reef.

The men on the pumps were fighting a losing battle, but they only gave up when the ship's carpenter reported that the keel was broken in two. There were several small boats nearby, but on a lee shore they dared not approach. The waves were now washing over the maindeck and the frigate was in danger of capsizing. But with no land in sight, the captain did not dare issue the order to abandon ship.

At dawn the following morning, they spotted the low shoreline of Anegada Island, less than a mile to the northwest. The crew had spent the night building rafts with wood hacked from the stricken ship. With some difficulty they launched them and made it to Anegada Island with the loss of four men. A boat with an officer and some seventy men landed on nearby Virgin Gorda, while the master, Mr McLean, and a number of men stayed on board in an attempt to salvage some of the stores and gear.

Two days later, HMS *St Christopher* turned up to rescue the crew. But a man named George Wright refused to leave the island. In the confusion he had stolen the captain's coat and had sold it to an Anegadian for two guineas. He accused the captain of running the *Astrea* aground through negligence, and called him 'a damned rascal'. He made a lunge for the captain's sword to stab him with it, but was restrained and taken to the waiting boat. The captain and his officers were exonerated by a court martial held aboard HMS *Ramillies*, off Barbados. George Wright was found

> **The captain turned hard to port, but it was too late: the *Astrea* struck the reef and began taking on water**

guilty of 'riotous and mutinous conduct' and hanged from the yardarm of another of His Majesty's ships. The wreck of the *Astrea* was rediscovered in 1967. Some small items were salvaged, but the ship's timbers, anchor and cannon remain underwater off Pelican Point, Anegada.

Louisbourg harbour in Nova Scotia is also a graveyard for a number of French ships. The fifty-gun *Apollon* and the twenty-six-gun *Fidele* were scuttled there because there were too few men to man them when it was anticipated that the British would attack. Three more French warships were accidentally burnt before the British arrived. During the attack itself, the sixty-four-gun *Célèbre*, the seventy-four-gun *Entreprenant* and the sixty-four-gun *Capricieux* were sunk on 21 July 1758, while the seventy-four-gun *Prudent* went down on 25 July in fifteen feet of water off Careening Point. Records show that some twenty-six ships sank in or near Louisbourg harbour between 1713 and 1758. A detailed survey of the site has now been completed and the wrecks of the *Célèbre*, the *Entreprenant*, the *Capricieux* and the *Prudent* have been located.

British Wars with America

When the British were not fighting the French, they were fighting the Americans. In 1776, British forces met rebels in the Battle of Valcour Island on Lake Champlain. The British had a resounding victory, sinking the traiterous Brigadier General Benedict Arnold's purpose-built gunboat, the *Philadelphia*, before it could close to fire. In 1935, New York salvage engineer Lorenzo F. Hagglund found the wreck perfectly preserved under fifty-six feet of the lake's cold, fresh water, with a British twenty-four-pound cannon ball still lodged in her bow. The *Philadelphia's* own gun, a Swedish twelve-pound smooth bore a hundred years older than the ship, was no match for the British weaponry. Hagglund raised the *Philadelphia*, mounted her on a barge and sailed around Lake Champlain for the next twenty-five years as a tourist attraction. When he died in 1961, the *Philadelphia* was acquired by the Smithsonian National Museum of American History in Washington, DC, where she is on permanent display. In 1997, another American gunboat, the *Spitfire*, nearly identical to the *Philadelphia*, was found in Lake Champlain.

During the British effort to retake Philadelphia in 1777, the sixty-four-gun HMS *Augusta* tried to force her way up the Delaware River. But she ran aground off Fort Mifflin while trying to avoid underwater obstacles placed in the Delaware River by the rebels. Pounded by artillery from the shore, the *Augusta* eventually caught fire. The crew abandoned ship and were rescued. At noon on 23 October 1777, the magazine exploded and the hulk then floated to the middle of the channel, where it sank. The *Augusta* was the largest British vessel lost in the American War of Independence. In 1849, her wreck was raised and towed to the New Jersey shore, where it became a tourist attraction. Bits were sold off but, exposed to air, the

The gunboat Philadelphia, *salvaged from Lake Champlain and now on display in the Smithsonian Museum*

timbers began to deteriorate, so the remaining good wood was stripped from the wreck and used to panel a room in the national headquarters of the Daughters of the American Revolution in Washington, DC.

In June 1779, the British began building Fort George on the top of a hill at Castine, Maine, in Penobscot Bay. The Americans reacted by massing men and warships in Boston. Around four hundred Continental Marines and a thousand militiamen were carried on thirty-seven vessels and arrived off Castine on 24 July 1779. They laid siege to the fort, but failed to take it before a superior British naval force turned up and blockaded them in Penobscot Bay. The American expedition then fled up the Penobscot

River, pursued by the British. The British captured two American warships and a number of transports, but the Americans decided to scuttle the rest before they were taken. The brig *Defence* was the last American boat left afloat. Cornered in Stockton Harbour, the crew set fire to the stern of the ship, where the magazine was located, and rowed ashore. The *Defence* blew up and sank. A detailed excavation of the ship began in 1975. It revealed that a hundred men lived on board the ship which was little more than a hundred feet long. Numerous mess tags were found. These were wooden pegs used to mark pieces of salt meat as they were cooked on a communal pot. The brick stove that was built around this large copper cauldron was also found. Although the American navy had no uniform at that time, a large number of buttons marked 'USA' were found, indicating either that soldiers had been seconded into the crew or that the crewmen had somehow acquired surplus army clothing. In all, on the Penobscot Expedition, the Americans lost 140 cannon and 450 men, the British only seventy. The naval commander of the expedition, Commodore Dudley Saltonstall, was drummed out of the navy. The army commanders were Colonel Paul Revere, who was court-martialled but acquitted, and Brigadier General Peleg Wadsworth, who was severely reprimanded. A hundred years later, Wadsworth's grandson, the poet Henry Wadsworth Longfellow turned Revere into a national hero with his poem 'The Midnight Ride of Paul Revere'.

The climax of the War of Independence occurred at Yorktown, where in October 1781 the British, under General Cornwallis, were under siege. HMS *Charon*, the largest of Cornwallis's warships, was at anchor in the York River on the night of 10 October, when she was hit by red-hot shot from a French cannon and caught fire. She drifted across the river, setting fire to several other ships on the way, before sinking. In 1978, she was rediscovered. Although only 5 per cent of her hull

survived it was possible to identify her from the original plans which were kept in the National Maritime Museum in Greenwich. Before Cornwallis surrendered on 19 October, numerous other ships were sunk, some scuttled to make shore defences. Several were refloated by the French, but twenty-six were unaccounted for. So far, nine wrecks in York River have been identified, including one thought to be of HMS *Fowey*.

Earlier in 1781, the seventy-four-gun HMS *Culloden* was being pursued by three French warships when, on 22 January, she was blown onto Shagwonggonac – or Shagwong – Reef. She was refloated and the captain tried to sail her into neighbouring Fort Pond Bay, but she sank off a headland later renamed Culloden Point. It seems that none of the six hundred men aboard were lost. Most of her guns and supplies were salvaged before the British burnt her to the water line. But part of the hull was still visible right up to the 1950s. Today, in twenty feet of water, several of her large guns and timbers can still be seen.

Though the Canadians stayed loyal to the British crown, British warships did not seem to have much luck in their waters either. In 1778, the twelve-gun HMS *Spy*, the sixteen-gun HMS *Cupid* and the thirty-two-gun HMS *Grampus* foundered off Newfoundland. HMS *Lynx* sank in the harbour at Halifax, Nova Scotia, during a gale on 26 September 1798. The sixty-four-gun HMS *Mars* had sunk there in June 1755 and a hurricane on 24 September 1757 sank the sixty-gun HMS *Tilbury* and the ten-gun HMS *Ferret* in Louisbourg harbour on Cape Breton Island. On 28 September 1798, HMS *Barbadoes* was wrecked on Sable Island, while the ten-gun HMS *Drake* was wrecked off Newfoundland on 20 June 1822 with a great loss of life.

The British and Americans were at war again in 1812. The fledgling United States were in danger of attack from Canada across the Great Lakes. On Lake Ontario, the sixteen-gun USS *Oneida* found herself up again the twenty-two-gun HMS *Royal*

George and five smaller warships. After a British attack on Sackets Harbour, New York, the American commander Captain Isaac Chauncey launched the twenty-four-gun *General Pike*, the twenty-gun *Madison* and the sixteen-gun *Sylph*. The British responded by building two twenty-four-gun warships, which were far superior to the American vessels. To counter this, Chauncey pressed into service two schooners, the *Hamilton* and the *Scourge*, seized British traders originally named the *Diana* and the *Lord Nelson* respectively. The *Hamilton* was fitted with ten cannon; the *Scourge* with eight. This made them dangerously top heavy.

'This craft was unfit for her duty, but time pressed, and no better offered,' said Ned Myers, a crewman on the *Scourge*. 'The bulwarks had been raised … [but] she was so tender that we could do little or nothing with her in a blow. It was often prognosticated that she would prove our coffin.'

For Myers this did not prove to be true, but it was for many of his crewmates. On 7 August 1813, the two squadrons were skirmishing in the lake. When evening came, they broke off. During the night a storm blew up and, hit by a sudden squall, the two top-heavy schooners capsized and sank in minutes. Myers jumped overboard, but others were trapped inside. He recalled seeing an officer struggle to get out of a stern window as the ship slipped below the surface. Myers found the ship's boat adrift and managed to save himself and a handful of shipmates, but most of those on the *Hamilton* and the *Scourge* perished.

The wrecks were found using a magnetometer in 1973. They are about 1,300 feet apart in some three hundred feet of water. A full investigation in 1980 by the inventor of the aqualung, Jacques Cousteau, revealed that the two ships were even then still in an astonishing state of preservation. The guns were still on their decks with powder ladles, rammers, cutlasses and boarding equipment lying alongside. The *Hamilton's* ship's boat was still hanging in its davits and the glass in *Scourge's* stern window was unbroken. The remains of five crewmen have also been spotted, including one skeleton tangled in the rigging that dragged the victim to his untimely, watery grave.

2 Iron Sinks

The USS *Cumberland* was the first victim of the new iron-clad, steam-powered ships of war. The 1,726-ton frigate was built in Boston navy yard and launched in May 1842. After seeing long service in the Mediterranean and in the US navy's Home and African Squadrons, she was in Gosport navy yard in Portsmouth, Virginia, when the Civil War broke out in 1861. The *Cumberland* escaped to sea when Gosport's commanding officer set fire to the yard. But the steam-powered USS *Merrimack* did not get out. Her crew set fire to her and she was scuttled at the dockside. While the well-armed *Cumberland* joined the US navy squadron blockading the entrance to the James River, Confederate engineers raised the *Merrimack*, and rebuilt her. They stripped her of her masts and installed a battery of guns under an iron casemate.

Standing out to sea on 8 March 1862, the *Merrimack*, now renamed the CSS *Virginia*, attacked the USS *Congress* which was part of the blockade. Shells from the *Congress's* guns simply bounced off the *Virginia's* armour, and the *Congress* fled, badly damaged. Next, the *Virginia* went after the *Cumberland*. Her captain Franklin Buchanan called for the *Cumberland* to surrender. Lieutenant George Morris, the *Cumberland's* executive officer in command, answered: 'Never. I'll sink alongside.' The *Virginia* then rammed her with a six-foot armoured ram that projected from her bow. As she went down, the *Cumberland* loosed off a broadside that damaged the ironclad and killed or wounded nine of her crew. In a matter of minutes the *Cumberland* had slipped below the waves, taking 120 of her crew with her.

The *Cumberland* was partially salvaged at the time, then left as a war grave. The wreck was redis-covered in 1981 lying in sixty-nine feet of water and added to America's National Register of Historic Places. However, she has been subjected to extensive dredging and looting since then. A number of artefacts from the *Cumberland* were recovered in police raids in March 1990 and four looters were prosecuted.

The firing of the Union dockyard at Norfolk, Virginia

The Confederate ironclad CSS Virginia *rams the USS* Cumberland, *8 March 1862*

Although both the French and the British had ironclads, the *Virginia* was the first to see action. But she did not have it all her own way for long. When the federal authorities heard that the Confederates were rebuilding the *Merrimack*, they commissioned an ironclad of their own, called the *Monitor*. Built in Brooklyn naval yard, she had a revolutionary new design devised by Swedish engineer John Ericsson and was said to look like a 'cheesebox on a raft'. To minimise the ship's profile, the deck rose only a few inches above the water line and the only superstructure was a revolving gun turret with two eleven-inch guns in it.

The *Monitor* arrived in the Hampton Roads off the James River the day after the *Cumberland* went down, and took on the *Virginia*. For four hours the two ironclads slugged it out. But their armour was more than a match for their armaments and little damage was inflicted. The action,

though, was seen as a watershed. Reporting the battle, *The Times* said that the strength of the Royal Navy had effectively been cut from 149 first-rate warships to two, her ironclads.

After this one indecisive bout, the *Monitor* stayed in Hampton Roads, but was given strict orders by President Lincoln not to engage the *Virginia* again. He feared that the loss of the *Monitor* might harm morale and jeopardise a planned attack on the Confederate capital, Richmond. That December, he ordered the *Monitor* to join the blockade of Charleston, to where she would be towed by the USS *Rhode Island*. The *Monitor's* revolutionary design may have protected her against bombardment, but it did not make her seaworthy. There was no seal around the bottom of the turret, so when heavy seas washed over her low decks they flooded her.

Inside, the machinery was connected to her

steam engine by leather belts. When these got wet they slipped off their shafts and the pumps stopped. On the evening of 30 December 1862, she lost her tow rope, leaving her wallowing hopelessly. Boats from the *Rhode Island* took off most of the crew, but there were still thirty-five on board when she sank at one o'clock the following morning.

As she went down, she turned over and the heavy turret came off. The upturned hull then landed on top of it in 246 feet of water. The wreck was located in 1973, and a full survey was carried out by the submersible *Johnson Sea Link* in 1977,

when divers recovered the red distress lamp that had been hung from her masthead before she went down. The wreck is now deteriorating quickly and efforts are being made to raise more of her.

During the American Civil War, the British gave covert aid to the Confederates. As part of this, the CSS *Alabama*, a 1,023-ton three-masted steam- and sail-powered barque, was built in John Laird's shipyard in Birkenhead, Liverpool, in 1862. She sailed for the Azores where she was fitted out as a Confederate raider under the command of Raphael Semmes. In the Atlantic waters she sank thirteen whalers and harassed other shipping. She

'The Wreck of the Iron-clad Monitor' Line engraving published in Harper's Weekly, *1863, depicting the USS* Monitor *sinking in a storm off Cape Hatteras on the night of 30-31 December 1862*

USS Kearsarge *vs.* CSS Alabama, *19 June 1864. This painting by Xanthus Smith, 1922, depicts* Alabama *sinking, at right, after her fight with the* Kearsarge *(seen at left)*

also operated in the Indian Ocean and the China Sea. On 11 January 1863, she caught up with the steamer USS *Hatteras* off Galveston, Texas and, after a twenty-minute battle, sank her. The order then went out to sink the *Alabama*.

In June 1864, after twenty-two months spent devastating United States' shipping, the *Alabama* put into Cherbourg to land prisoners and make use of the dry dock there. But she had been followed into French waters by the sloop of war USS *Kearsarge*. On 19 June, the two ships joined

battle. The *Alabama* was outgunned by the *Kearsarge* and not as strongly built. Semmes surrendered but, along with other officers and men, escaped capture when they were taken on board an English yacht which had been standing by. The *Alabama* sank in 190 feet of water.

With the aid of sonar, a French navy mine hunter located the wreck of the *Alabama* in October 1984, but investigating the wreck was a problem as it was essentially United States government property located in French territorial waters.

USS Cairo *destroyed by a Confederate mine, 12 December 1862*

1862, she went into action in support of Grant's siege of Vicksburg, steaming up the Yazoo River with a flotilla of other ironclads to attack the city's northern defences.

The Confederates, however, had some new technology of their own, namely the electrically detonated mine. As the *Cairo* engaged the Confederate shore batteries, she ran over a mine field. Two huge explosions ripped through her hull, whereupon water began to pour in 'like the roar of Niagara', as one survivor put it. Captain Thomas Selfridge quickly beached her and the crew scrambled ashore. The *Cairo* then slid back out into midstream and, after twelve minutes, sank.

Plans to raise her in 1864 and 1882 came to nothing. But in 1956, two local historians located her with the aid of a compass. In 1960, the armoured pilothouse was raised, along with the

An agreement between the two governments was signed in October 1989, and diving began, but in 1994, it was discovered that there was a live shell still in the barrel of one of the *Alabama's* Blakely guns. French bomb disposal experts had to be called in to defuse it. The remains of the ship's wheel were found with its brass bindings inscribed with the *Alabama's* ship's motto: *'Aide-toi et Dieu t'aidera'* – 'God helps those who help themselves'. Also found on board were Brazilian coins from the *Alabama's* visit to Bahia in 1863, kitchenware from Staffordshire, a soap box from Boston and the tooth of a sperm whale probably taken from one of the thirteen whalers she had sunk off the Azores.

The naval battles of the American Civil War were fought not just at sea but also on the Mississippi and its tributaries as the Union tried to strangle the Confederacy. For this riverine war, the Union built a series of gunboats, steam-driven and with a wooden hull for a shallow draught. Topside there was an angled iron casemate to protect the crew, the armaments and the paddle wheel.

One of these gunboats was the USS *Cairo*. Built by James B. Eads in 1862 in Mound City, Illinois, she was named for Cairo, Illinois, the headquarters of General Ulysses S. Grant during his western campaign. She was 175 feet long, fifty-one feet wide and displaced 888 tons. On 12 December

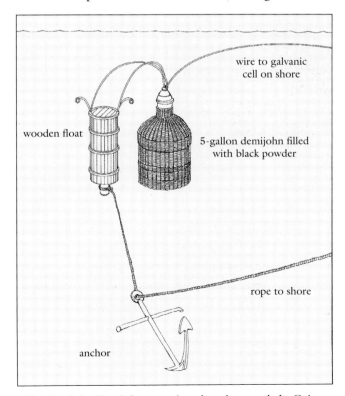

wire to galvanic cell on shore

wooden float

5-gallon demijohn filled with black powder

rope to shore

anchor

Sketch of the Confederate mine that destroyed the Cairo

Cairo's eight-inch naval gun which was still loaded. Then in 1964, an attempt to raise the hull was made, but the salvors had underestimated its weight and it broke into three parts when they lifted it. The bow was raised intact, but the midsection was crushed by the lifting cables and the stern fell back into the water along with many of the artefacts the wreck had contained. The surviving pieces were carried on a barge to Pascagoula, Mississippi, where they were left to rot, though the gun and some smaller artefacts were conserved by volunteers. Conservation of the body of the wreck only began in 1977, after title had passed from the State of Mississippi to the National Park Service. She is now on display outside under an open shelter, but marine archaeologists cite the raising of the *Cairo* as an object lesson in how not to recover a shipwreck.

Disaster on the Mississippi

One of the biggest ever nautical disasters happened at the end of the Civil War. At 2 am on 27 April 1865, the huge side-paddle steamer *Sultana* sank on the Mississippi. Some 1,547 died – exceeding even the 1,519 death toll lost on the *Titanic*. However, few people have ever heard of the sinking of the *Sultana* because news of the accident was overshadowed by one of the great events of history.

The *Sultana* had been launched two years before during the American Civil War as part of the Union's strategy to carry troops and supplies up and down the Ohio, Missouri and Mississippi Rivers. After the war ended, she was sailed to Vicksburg, Mississippi, to carry the Union soldiers who had been held prisoner at the Confederate prison camp at Andersonville back north to Cairo, Illinois.

Although only two years old, the *Sultana* was in a decrepit condition due to her war service: her scheduled overhaul was, however, postponed until after the prisoners of war could be returned. Most

of the men were already walking skeletons, and many had to be carried on stretchers, but they were naturally all extremely eager to get home. The *Sultana's* capacity was just 376, but that day she carried 2,200 people, along with sixty horses and mules, and a hundred hogs.

On 27 April 1865, she had just passed Memphis and was fighting the strong current of the Mississippi when she was rocked by a huge explo-

sion, quickly followed by two more. One of the *Sultana's* boilers had blown up. A column of fire and steam shot up almost cutting the boat in two and flames engulfed the vessel. Few of those who had survived the original explosions were strong enough to swim and those who did not die in the conflagration on board, drowned.

The *Sultana* was skippered by maverick captain J Cass Mason who had just won the distinction of making the fastest trip between New Orleans and St Louis. He had arrived in Vicksburg a few weeks before on his way to New Orleans and had met the chief quartermaster of the Mississippi, Colonel Ruben Heath, who told him that the federal

The Mississippi steamer Sultana. *Her loss on 27 April 1865 would become America's worst peacetime disaster to that date*

government was offering to pay $5 per enlisted man and $10 per officer to any steamboat operator who would take them back to the north. Heath was a scoundrel who had been cheating the government throughout the war and had only managed to avoid court-martial through his family connections in Washington. Mason left for New Orleans while Heath arranged to collect together as many men as he could for him to pick up on the return trip.

Heath approached the officer in charge of prisoner repatriation, Captain Frederick Speed, using bribes and deception. Speed in turn contacted Captains Williams and Kerns who were under pressure to empty their transit camps. When the *Sultana* returned to Vicksburg, over 1,400 men were ready to board and more were arriving by train.

The *Sultana* was delayed slightly when she developed a bulge and leak in one of her four boilers. Engineers advised the captain to have two plates removed and replaced, but Cass made do with riveting a metal patch over the defect. Boarding began on the morning of 24 April. Some of the men on board expressed their worries that she was being overloaded, on seeing crew wedging large beams under decks that were beginning to sag due to weight of passengers. They were also puzzled that so many were boarding the *Sultana* when there were other craft available.

As the boat cast off from Vicksburg docks, the *Sultana* was carrying nearly 2,100 former prisoners of war, escorted by twenty-two men of the Fifty-eighth Ohio Regiment. Added to this there were ninety or so paying passengers and a crew of eighty-eight – all on board a boat licensed to carry fewer than four hundred people. The *Sultana's* cargo holds also carried two thousand hogsheads of sugar, each weighing 1,200 lb, and more bizarrely, a large alligator in a crate which Mason

> **The escaping steam scalded everyone in its path and flung them into the river, which was, at least, a little cooler**

had bought in New Orleans, intending to keep as a mascot.

The first signs of trouble arose when the boat passed other vessels or sights of interest on the shore. As men moved from side to side she listed badly, resulting in the water in her boilers sloshing about from one side to the other, emptying the boilers on one side and flooding those on the other side. Then as the boat righted, steam pressure built up in the boilers that were refilling. The crew tried to stop the men of the Fifty-eighth moving about, but the list got worse when the sugar was unloaded at Memphis. Without this acting as ballast the boat became even more top heavy.

A few men had slipped ashore and disappeared after helping to unload the sugar, but overcrowding was still a problem as the *Sultana* slipped her moorings at around midnight on the 26th. Seven miles upstream she hit a full flood current and heeled further. The patched starboard boiler could no longer take the pressure and blew, followed by the two boilers amidships. The blast tore out the centre of the vessel, ripping apart the upper decks. The area immediately above the boiler room where the sick and wounded had been lying was completely destroyed.

The escaping steam caused horrific injuries. As it blasted aft, it scalded everyone in its path and flung them into the river. Then one of the huge smoke stacks came crashing down causing more carnage. The damaged furnaces set fire to the ship and the flames were fanned by the breeze blowing down the river.

At first the men in the bow area thought they were safe as the fire spread aft. But the wreck turned in the current and the fire spread towards them. They flung anything that would float overboard and jumped in after, or lowered themselves into the water on ropes. Months of poor food and deprivation in Confederate prisons meant that many were too weak to swim and they drowned. One quick-thinking soldier saved himself making a makeshift life raft: Private William Lugenbeal bayoneted Captain Mason's alligator and clambered aboard its crate, which carried him downstream to safety.

An hour after the blast, the southbound steamer *Boston II* came upon the burning *Sultana* and pulled some 150 survivors from the water. She then sped downstream to Memphis where the captain raised the alarm. But the town was already aware of the accident. Private Wesley Lee had been blown off the deck and was carried downstream to Memphis where he was spotted by night-watchmen on the levee. Numerous small craft took to the water to search for survivors. However, soldiers on guard at the nearby Fort Pickering had been told to be on watch for guerrilla activity and opened fire on the boats. Fortunately, nobody was injured and, once the situation was made clear, the soldiers joined the rescue.

Some forty or so men saved themselves by lowering themselves into the water and hanging onto the hull. When most of the *Sultana's* superstructure had burnt away, they climbed back on board again. The wreck drifted into a flooded grove of trees where, shortly after the men were taken off, she sank. In all 786 people were rescued, most of whom were injured in some way. Some two hundred of these would die later in hospital. Captain Mason was among the dead, killed when the pilothouse and the officers' quarters were destroyed by the initial blast. The survivors continued their journey on another steamer. Understandably, many were reluctant to make the trip: one man spent the entire journey sitting in the steamer's dinghy.

The sinking of the *Sultana* was the worst waterborne disaster in American history, but received comparatively little publicity, overshadowed as it was by other events. The day before the tragedy occurred, John Wilkes Booth, the man who assassinated Abraham Lincoln, had been cornered and killed. The hunt for the other conspirators was still on, so the story of the *Sultana* disaster was relegated to a few paragraphs on the back pages of the nation's newspapers and soon forgotten.

In all, there were three official investigations into the *Sultana* disaster. At first it was suspected that a Confederate bomb had been smuggled on board in the coal, but engineers quickly dismissed this theory. Clearly other factors were to blame. Maritime experts singled out the poorly designed boilers that had been badly repaired, the top-heavy state of the craft and the lack of ballast.

Four men were blamed for the overcrowding: Colonel Heath and Captains Speed, Williams and Kerns. Williams and Kerns, although in charge of the prisoners' transportation, managed to escape official censure. Heath had quit the army soon after the disaster and was beyond the jurisdiction of the military court, so Speed became the scapegoat at the subsequent court-martial. His defence tried to subpoena the unscrupulous Heath, but he refused to testify and, as he was no longer a soldier, he could not be forced to do so. Speed was found guilty on all counts and faced a dishonourable discharge. However, the Judge Advocate General of the Army reviewed the case and reversed the findings. No one else was ever charged.

There is no memorial to the soldiers who died. Survivors sought to have one erected, but their efforts came to nothing as the public wanted to put the war behind them. Their only memorial is a literary one. Major Will McTeer, the adjutant of the Third Tennessee Cavalry, which lost 213 men in the catastrophe, wrote:

'There in the bosom of the Mississippi they found their resting place. No stone or tablet marked with their names or even unknown for them… flowers are strewn over the graves in the cemeteries of our dead but there are none for the men who went down with the *Sultana*. But let us remember them.'

The Early Ironclads

Off Daniel's Head in Bermuda, the wreck of the Royal Navy's first twin-screw warship HMS *Vixen* can be seen protruding from the water where she was scuttled in 1896. Launched in 1864, *Vixen* was a new type of ship called an armoured gunboat, with an iron frame and armour plating inside to protect the engine, magazine, armaments and crew, but an outer hull of teak: when iron gets cold, it becomes brittle and can shatter easily, whereas wood is flexible and can withstand bombardment better.

With a top speed of just over nine knots, the *Vixen* and her sister ships were the slowest iron-clads in the Navy. Her bunkers carried only enough coal for twelve days' steaming, so she had a full set of masts and sails. Her telescopic funnel retracted when she was under sail and her screws were lifted.

She was not very seaworthy and was almost lost in a gale in the Irish Sea in 1867. The following year she was towed to Bermuda. When it became clear in 1873 that she was going to be stationed there permanently, her masts and rigging were removed. Stripped of her guns, she was sunk to block Chubb Cut Channel twenty-three years later.

Marine technology was developing fast, however, and armoured gunboats were quickly replaced by steel-hulled battleships. One of the first was the USS *Massachusetts*. Commissioned in 1896, she was protected by a belt of nickel case-hardened steel up to eighteen inches thick and her ten-thousand-horsepower engine meant she could cruise at a top speed of fifteen knots. Displacing ten thousand tons, she was 350 feet long and carried two thirteen-inch gun batteries, four eight-inch batteries, four torpedo tubes and a host of smaller ordinance.

Commemorative postcard of the USS Maine, *before she exploded and sank in Havana harbour, sparking a war*

She first saw action off Cuba in 1898 during the Spanish-American war. At the time, America was expanding into an imperial power, taking Puerto Rico and the Philippines as overseas territories. But in 1906, the British had launched HMS *Dreadnought* with ten twelve-inch guns and a top speed of twenty-one knots. The *Massachusetts* – once the leading example of marine technology – was now out of date. She was laid up, but in 1910 she was refitted, modernised and went back into service. Decommissioned again in 1914, she was returned to service once more when the United States entered World War I in 1917, and was used for gunnery practice. But by 1919, her active duty was over. In 1921, she was loaned to the War Department as a target for coastal artillery practice. Stripped of her guns, she was towed to Pensacola, where she was scuttled. Hit by over a hundred rounds of artillery fire, she was left to rot until 1956, when commercial salvage companies sought to raise her for scrap. Local people objected and the Supreme Court awarded title to the State of Florida. She became a State Underwater Archaeological Preserve on 10 June 1993, the centenary of her launch.

The Spanish-American War began with the sinking of the USS *Maine* in the harbour at Havana, where she had been stationed to protect US citizens following anti-Spanish riots on Cuba, at the time beginning its struggle for independence from Spain. On 15 February 1868, the *Maine* exploded, killing 260 seamen: a Spanish mine was blamed. The Spanish protested their innocence, but US newspapers whipped up war fever with the slogan: 'Remember the *Maine*, to hell with Spain.'

It was only in 1911 that the wreck was inspected after a coffer dam was built around it. It soon became apparent that the *Maine* had been sunk by an internal explosion. A second investigation in 1976 concluded that a fire in the coal bunker had ignited the magazine. The stern, which was intact, was towed out to deep water where it was sunk in 1912. The rest of its wreckage has been removed.

The *Maine's* forward turret remained in Havana as a memorial, while the ship's bell, anchor and foremast form the memorial to the crew in the US National Cemetery at Arlington.

The North Sea is littered with the wrecks of warships from World War I. *The Blücher* lies on Dogger Bank. HMS *Pathfinder* lies off the Firth of Forth. There are a number of wrecks from the Battle of Jutland, the only major engagement between the British and German fleets, and the wrecks of numerous U-boats have been located, including that of *U-20* which sank the *Lusitania*.

The *Mont Blanc*

One of the biggest maritime disasters of the war took place on the other side of the Atlantic in the harbour at Halifax, Nova Scotia. On 6 December 1917, the Norwegian vessel *Imo* ran into the *Mont Blanc*, a French freighter loaded with 5,000 tons of explosives. The collision set off the French ship's cargo, in an explosion that was felt over sixty miles away. The blast killed 1,635 people.

Halifax was Canada's major wartime port. Troops and supplies were loaded for the perilous journey across the Atlantic to England where they were mustered before being moved on to France. In December 1917, the harbour was packed with shipping, which included the cruiser HMS *Highflyer* and the SS *Imo*, which had 'Belgium Relief' on her sides to emphasise her neutrality to U-boats and was on her way to New York to load relief supplies for Belgium.

The previous evening, the *Mont Blanc* had arrived from New York, where she was loaded with a cocktail of explosives and volatile material. The ship had her holds lined with wood held together with non-sparking copper nails. But she was overloaded and was carrying 2,300 tons of wet and dry picric acid, used for making lyddite for artillery shells; two hundred tons of TNT; ten tons of gun cotton and drums of Bezol – high octane fuel – stacked on her decks.

She arrived off Halifax on the evening of 5 December 1917. But it was too late to be let through the anti-submarine nets, and she had to wait until the next day to enter the harbour. On the morning of the 6 December, the *Imo* weighed anchor and headed out of the harbour, just as the *Mont Blanc* was coming in. They collided in the bottleneck known as the 'Narrows'. Some of the Bezol drums the *Mont Blanc* was carrying broke loose. Fuel spilt on the deck and caught fire. Knowing the ship was a bomb, Captain Le Medec ordered all hands to abandon ship and jumped over the side himself. Unmanned and on fire, the *Mont Blanc* drifted towards Halifax harbour where she ran into pier six in the staging area.

At 9.05 am, the *Mont Blanc* went up. The whole ship disintegrated in a massive explosion that killed over 1,500 people instantly, including eight of the crew of HMS *Highflyer*. The blast flattened the buildings for two square miles. In all, an area of 325 acres was devastated and most of the windows in Halifax were blown out. Many spectators suffered eye injuries from the flying glass.

A mushroom-shaped cloud rose several miles into the sky, and three thousand tons of debris rained down on Halifax. The waters of the Narrows seemed to boil with shrapnel from the ship and falling rocks which had been sucked up from the harbour bed. The ship's gun landed near Alboro Lake a mile-and-a-half away, while the stock of one of her anchors landed in a wood three miles away.

The blast caused a manmade tsunami that rocked nearby ships at their moorings and overwhelmed some smaller vessels. The wave then travelled across to the shores of Dartmouth, where it was funnelled into Tufts cove and washed away a settlement of the Micmac, the native American tribe of the area.

The blast set fire to many of the wooden houses, and others were set ablaze by overturned stoves.

The fire soon threatened the naval magazine at the Wellington Barracks and the area was evacuated of civilians, until the magazine was finally made safe by dumping its contents into the harbour. Afterwards, rescuers returned to the city but their efforts were hampered by nightfall and the onset of a blizzard.

Rumours spread that Halifax was being bombed by Zeppelins, or that it had been on the receiving end of a German naval bombardment. Anti-German hysteria ran high, and survivors with German-sounding names were attacked. As it was, the port of Halifax was put out of operation, which had a devastating effect on the war effort.

Many civilians suffered burns, blindness and other injuries as a result of the explosion. The Halifax Relief Commission was established to help the injured, the bereaved and those made homeless by the accident. This organisation is still aiding the remaining survivors of the disaster, over eighty years after the explosion.

Funds poured in from around the world, even from as far away as New Zealand. However, most of the relief came from the state of Massachusetts which sent not only doctors, nurses, medical supplies, food and clothing, but also transport, glass and glaziers. Every year Halifax presents Boston with a giant Christmas tree to express its thanks.

Under the terms of the Armistice ending World War I in 1918, the German High Seas Fleet was interned in Scapa Flow, the Royal Navy's anchorage off the north of Scotland. However, rumours spread that through the peace talks in Versailles, the German fleet was to be handed over to the British. So on 21 June 1919 the German commander Rear Admiral Ludwig von Reuter ordered his men to scuttle their ships. The British managed to beach some of them, but fifty-nine of seventy-four German ships at anchor went down. Between 1923 and 1939 an effort was made to salvage them. Only

At 9.05 am on 6 December 1917 the *Mont Blanc* went up in a massive explosion, killing over 1,500 people

seven remain – the cruisers *Brummer, Dresden, Karlsruhe* and *Köln*, and the battleships *König, Markgraf* and *Kronprinz Wilhelm*.

There are other wrecks in Scapa Flow. On 13 October 1939, a German U-boat penetrated the defences and torpedoed the British battleship *Royal Oak*. She sank quickly with the loss of 833 in thirty-three feet of water. A designated war grave, diving is not allowed on the site.

After World War I, naval treaties were signed to prevent the Germans building battleships of over ten thousand tons. This heralded the invention of the pocket battleship. In 1937, the *Admiral Graf Spee* was launched in Wilhelmshaven. It was named after a heroic German admiral who died when his fleet was destroyed by the British in the Battle of

the Falklands in 1914. In fact the Germans were already breaching their treaty obligations and the *Graf Spee* actually displaced twelve thousand tons. Aluminium was used for its superstructure and interior and the hull was welded rather than riveted to save weight. Powered by four two-stroke diesel engines, she had a top speed of 28.5 knots and carried six 280mm guns housed in two revolving turrets, eight 150mm guns on pivot mounts, six 105mm anti-aircraft guns, eight 37mm light anti-aircraft guns, and twelve 20mm anti-aircraft machine guns, along with eight torpedo tubes, two catapult-launched reconnaissance aircraft and a battle crew of 1,188.

On 21 August 1939, shortly before the outbreak of World War II, the *Graf Spee* slipped

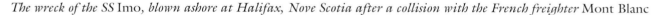

The wreck of the SS Imo, *blown ashore at Halifax, Nove Scotia after a collision with the French freighter* Mont Blanc

The German pocket battleship Graf Spee *burns off Uruguay. The ship was scuttled by her captain after a battle with the British cruisers* Ajax, Achilles *and* Exeter *on 13 December 1939*

out of Wilhelmshaven under the command of Captain Hans Langsdorff. When Britain and France declared war on Germany on 3 September, Langsdorff was in the South Atlantic. On 26 September, he got orders to hunt down commercial shipping. Four days later he stopped the British freighter *Clement* and sank her after getting the crew off first. He sank eight more British merchant ships with no loss of life. But the British were determined to put a stop to the *Graf Spee*. They sent twenty-three capital ships badly needed for other duties to track her down. On 13 December, three British cruisers – *Ajax*, *Achilles* and *Exeter* – caught up with her off the mouth of the River Plate where she was waiting to ambush a British convoy. Although heavily outgunned, the British attacked. The *Exeter* was put out of action with more than fifty casualties. *Ajax* was also hit.

But the furious British attack had also inflicted damage on the *Graf Spee* which pulled into Montevideo.

The British put pressure on the Uruguayan government and Langsdorff was given just four days to make repairs and bury his dead. Meanwhile HMS *Cumberland* arrived in the Plate. On 17 December, Langsdorff put to sea again, but three miles out he scuttled his ship. He and his men escaped to Argentina, which was more sympathetic to the German cause. Three days later he lay down on the old German Imperial Navy flag in his hotel room in Buenos Aires and shot himself.

The wreck of the *Graf Spee* was surveyed in 1997. It was badly damaged and there was evidence that the British had salvaged some of her equipment soon after she went down. The Uruguayan navy raised one of her 150mm guns which is now on display in a park in Montevideo.

Sink the *Bismarck!*

The other pride of the German fleet was the *Bismarck*. She had been built after a new naval treaty was signed, restricting German battleship displacement to 35 per cent of that of the Royal Navy. Her planned displacement was 35,000 tons but when she was launched on 14 February 1939 it had crept up to 44,734 tons. The true displacements of the *Bismarck* and her sister ship *Tirpitz* were kept secret until Germany capitulated in May 1945.

In May 1941, the *Bismarck* went out to sea with the heavy cruiser *Prinz Eugen* to attack Atlantic convoys. They were spotted by the *Prince of Wales* and the *Hood*, both of which joined battle. The action lasted sixteen minutes. A shell from the *Bismarck* hit the *Hood's* aft magazine and she blew up. Only three of her crew of 1,418 survived. The *Prince of Wales* was also damaged, but so was the *Bismarck*. Churchill gave the order that the Royal Navy must sink the *Bismarck* at any cost.

Taking on water, the *Bismarck* made for St Nazaire – then in German hands – to make repairs.

The cruiser *Repulse*, the battleship *King George V* and the aircraft carrier *Victorious* were soon in hot pursuit. Staying out of range of the Bismarck's guns, *Victorious* launched eight Swordfish torpedo planes which inflicted more damage. But the *Bismarck* managed to evade her pursuers and disappeared for thirty-two hours. On 26 May, she was spotted by a flying boat. More Swordfishes attacked from the *Ark Royal* and one of their torpedoes hit the *Bismarck's* rudder and jammed her steering gear.

On the morning of 27 May, the battleships *King George V* and *Rodney*, escorted by the heavy cruisers *Dorsetshire* and *Norfolk*, caught up with her. Over the next eighty-eight minutes, the *Royal Navy* fired 2,876 shells at the *Bismarck*. As many as four hundred hit her. Five or six torpedoes also struck the ship. As she blazed, the crew abandoned ship and when she began to roll over, the *Dorsetshire* fired one more torpedo into her. At 10.40 pm she slipped beneath the waves. Of her crew of 2,206, only 110 were picked up. More would have been saved, but the sighting of a submarine forced the British ships to withdraw, leaving men in the water. Another three men made it home, after they were rescued from a raft by a U-boat.

In June 1989, the wreck of the *Bismarck* was found in fifteen thousand feet of water some four hundred miles off Brest. Cameras were sent down to examine her and, although all the superstructure had been destroyed, she was remarkably intact for a ship that had taken so much punishment. There were furrows in her steel deck where British shells had hit. The survey also found evidence confirming earlier German reports that the *Bismarck* had been scuttled at the last moment.

On 13 November 1941, the Germans got their revenge on *Ark Royal* as she was returning from Malta where she had taken a consignment of aircraft. At 3.41 pm she was hit by a torpedo under the bridge on the starboard side, causing serious damage. Within three minutes she was listing by

Death of a battleship: the Bismarck, *battered by shells and torpedoes, finally gives up the ghost. The ship performed a complete roll to port as she sank before righting herself to settle in an upright position on the bottom of the Atlantic*

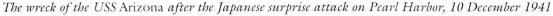

twelve degrees. The starboard engine room was out of action, but the port and central engine rooms were still working – a mix-up many have suggested contributed to her loss. The order had been given to transfer the ship's company to HMS *Legion* and many key engine room and damage control personnel had been evacuated when she could, perhaps, have been saved. But it was impossible to get them back. Soon the centre and port boiler rooms flooded. Electric power failed. At 6.15 pm the destroyer HMS *Laforey* came alongside to supply power, but the destroyer's officers did not know their way around *Ark Royal* and could not connect their power lines to the pumps. A tug began to tow her towards Gibraltar and at midnight steam was raised in one boiler. But at 2.15 am on the 14th a fire broke out in the port boiler room. In fifteen minutes, her list had increased to thirty-five degrees and she had to be abandoned. She sank twenty-nine miles east of Gibraltar at 6.13 am.

Pearl Harbor

On 7 December 1941, the Japanese attacked the American Pacific Fleet at its base in Pearl Harbor. There were some 3,400 casualties, with 2,403 killed, including 68 civilians. 169 aircraft were completely destroyed and 150 damaged. Most were still on the ground. The battleship *Arizona* was hit by eight bombs. She exploded and sank. Of the 1,177 men on board, only two hundred survived. The *Oklahoma* was hit by several torpedoes and capsized, while the *Nevada*, *California*, and *West Virginia* sank in shallow water. Three other battleships, three cruisers, three destroyers and several smaller vessels were badly damaged.

Although the attack on Pearl Harbor seemed

The wreck of the USS Arizona *after the Japanese surprise attack on Pearl Harbor, 10 December 1941*

The USS Arizona *memorial at Pearl Harbor, built across the central section of the battleship*

like a crushing defeat for the US, the carrier fleet was at sea and escaped any damage, and with the exception of the *Arizona* and the *Oklahoma* all the other ships sunk that day were repaired and returned to service. Plans were laid for the wreck of the *Oklahoma* to be removed, but first she had to be righted. A series of 'headframes' – forty-foot towers were built along the side of the capsized ship. Cables passed over them were attached to twenty-one electric winches on shore. The hull was sealed and pumped full of compressed air.

Then she was gradually righted. This took until June 1943.

There were no plans to raise the *Arizona*. Pictures of the blacked-out ship had become a potent symbol of the attack on Pearl Harbor around the world. During the war she served as a potent propaganda tool, since when her wreck has been left as a shrine to the memory to all those who died that day. The superstructure was removed and, in 1962, a memorial designed by architect Alfred Preis was built over the wreck which lies just below the surface of the water, where it is visited by over five thousand people each day.

A popular belief during the war was that a bomb had fallen down the funnel and exploded her boilers. In fact, she was sunk by a huge bomb modified from a sixteen-inch shell which penetrated her deck and detonated her forward magazine. Even so it is amazing how much of the wreck is intact. Divers surveying the wreck in 1983 found clothes in the lockers and unbroken light bulbs.

The war in the Pacific littered the seabed with wrecks. More than fifty US, Australian, New Zealand and Japanese ships went down during the fighting on Guadalcanal. The waterway off the island is now called Iron Bottom Sound because of the amount of wreckage there. It was surveyed in 1991 and ten wrecks were found, including those of the HMAS *Canberra*, the US cruisers *Atlanta*, *Northampton* and *Quincy*, the US destroyers *Aaron Ward*, *Barton*, *Cushing*, *DeHaven*, *Laffey* and *Monssen*, the Japanese destroyers *Ayanami* and *Yudachi*, and the Japanese battleship *Kirishima*. The bow of the US battleship *Minneapolis* has also been found, along with oilers, transports, a Japanese submarine, a New Zealand corvette, landing barges, the US tug *Seminole* and aircraft, including American and Japanese fighters, a Kawanishi flying boat and a B-17 'Flying Fortress'. Almost everything found was badly damaged by shells and torpedoes.

During the Battle of Midway, 4-6 June 1942, the US carrier *Yorktown* was hit below the water line by two torpedoes and the order to abandon ship was given. But she did not go down. After the battle, she was being towed back to Pearl Harbor by a minesweeper when, soon after dawn on 6 June, a Japanese submarine torpedoed her again and sank one of her destroyer escorts, the *Hannan*. The *Yorktown* stayed afloat until the early hours of 7 June, when she suddenly rolled over and plunged to the bottom of the Pacific.

Her wreck was found in 1998. A robotic

exploration showed that she was remarkably intact. The wooden flight deck was still in place, there was paint on her hull and her anti-aircraft guns were still pointing skywards.

Japan's own Pearl Harbor was the Pacific atoll of Truk, where the Japanese Fourth Fleet was based. The US navy attacked it on 16-17 February and 29-30 April 1944. There were also frequent raids with B-24s and B-25s and the British Royal Navy gave it another pounding on 16 June 1945. Truk was even considered a suitable target for the atomic bomb, then under development. As it is, more than forty-three Japanese ships lie under the water at Truk. These include four destroyers, three light cruisers, a patrol boat, a seaplane tender and numerous smaller craft.

Since the war Japanese groups have gone to great lengths to removed human remains from the wrecks. In 1971, the government of Truk declared the lagoon a National Marine Sanctuary. Diving is encouraged on the wrecks, though it is illegal to remove artefacts.

Testing the Atom Bomb

The *Prinz Eugen*, which had partnered the *Bismarck* but become separated from her, survived the war and surrendered to the British in Copenhagen on 7 May 1945. Turned over to the United States, she joined a fleet of 242 ships at Bikini Atoll which served as target ships in a series of atomic bomb tests. Surviving two bomb blasts, the *Prinz Eugen* was taken to Kwajalein atoll where she was examined for the effects of blast and radiation. She developed leaks and, on 22 December 1946, rolled over and sank on a reef off Enubuj Island, to the northwest, where her stern can still be seen jutting from the water. These atom bomb tests, known as Operation Crossroads, sank numerous enemy ships and obsolete alien vessels at Bikini and Kwajalein.

In 1989, the US National Park Service sent divers to examine the wrecks. The USS *Gilliam* was found in 180 feet of water. She had been hit by the fireball of a twenty-kiloton airburst which blew off her superstructure and warped her hull. She sank in seventy-nine seconds.

The USS *Carlisle* had been a little further away. She was thrown 150 feet. Her superstructure was pushed sideways. Her deck was compressed and her plates were dished and buckled.

The USS *Arkansas* survived the first blast but capsized when a second 20-kiloton bomb was detonated 90 feet below the surface, creating a tidal wave. It lies upside down in 180 feet of water. Reports said it went straight to the bottom.

The USS *Saratoga* was inundated by the fountain of water blasted into the air by the explosion. This smashed her flight deck and buckled her hull. Even so, it took her seven-and-a-half hours to sink. The divers found no trace of the five aircraft that had been strapped to her deck, but four planes remained intact in her hangars. The *Saratoga*'s anti-aircraft guns, torn from their mountings by the blast, lie on the seabed nearby.

The rudder and screw of the German heavy cruiser Prinz Eugen, *off Enubuj Island, where she struck a reef and sank*

3 Treasure Ships

On 4 September 1622, a Spanish treasure fleet sailed from Havana, loaded with gold and silver mined in Spain's New World possessions of Peru, Ecuador, Venezuela, Mexico and Columbia, copper from Cuba and indigo from Peru. Holland had recently declared against Spain in the Thirty Years' War, which had been raging across Europe since 1618, and the Dutch fleet had joined French and English pirates in attacking Spanish vessels.

A large Dutch fleet was in the area and extra precautions were taken. The fleet's commander, the Marquis of Cardereita, sailed in the lead ship of the guard fleet, the *Nuestra Señora de Candeleria*. The bulk of the treasure was split between the *Santa Margarita* and the *Nuestra Señora de Atocha* and as the *Atocha* had been outfitted with twenty bronze cannon, she would sail as a rearguard to protect the slower merchant ships. In all, there were twenty-eight ships in the fleet as they slipped out of port.

One day out of Havana, the weather turned bad: a hurricane was approaching. As the sky darkened and heavy rain cut visibility, the ships became separated. In the heavy sea, the ships rolled violently and the passengers and crew of the *Atocha* watched in horror as the smaller *Nuestra Señora de Consolacion* capsized and sank.

That night the wind shifted, pushing the fleet north towards Florida. By dawn, the *Candeleria* and twenty other ships had managed to get to the west of the Dry Tortugas and were able to ride out the storm in the Gulf of Mexico. But the rest were being blown onto the Florida Keys. Fifteen-foot rollers ground the *Santa Margarita* into the shallows of a low-lying atoll, fringed with mangrove swamps. Her commander, Captain Bernardino de Lugo, could see the *Atocha* to the east, but could only watch helplessly as the crew of the *Atocha* dropped anchors in a desperate attempt to keep her off a reef. In vain: the huge sea lifted the *Atocha* and smashed her onto it. The mainmast snapped and she was holed in the bow. She quickly filled with water and went down leaving only the stump of the mizzenmast above the waves.

Of the 265 people on board, only three crewmen and two black slaves survived. They were found clinging to the mast next morning and were rescued by the *Santa Cruz*. In all, 550 people were dead. Cargo worth over two million pesos was lost and the rest of the treasure fleet was scattered over fifty miles. Twenty of the twenty-eight ships limped back to Havana.

A salvage fleet of five ships under Gaspar de Vargas was sent out to find the *Atocha* and the *Santa Margarita*. With her shattered mizzenmast still rising out of the water, the *Atocha* was easily located where she had sunk in fifty-five feet of water. At that depth it was difficult for divers without breathing apparatus to work. To make things more difficult still, all the hatches and gun ports were securely fastened, and all the divers could salvage were two small iron swivel cannon found on the deck.

Vargas then sailed west in search of the *Santa Margarita*. There was no sign of her, but at Loggerhead Key he found the *Rosario* and rescued a small group of survivors. Unable to refloat her, Vargas burned the *Rosario* to the water line, exposing her cargo for salvage.

In early October a second hurricane hit, curtailing salvage operations and Vargas returned to Havana to get equipment to salvage the *Atocha*. But when they returned to the place where they had last seen her she had disappeared. The second hurricane had moved her. They dragged the bottom with grappling hooks but found nothing.

The following February, the Marquis of Cardereita joined the salvage team. A few silver ingots were raised, but they could not find the hull. In August they gave up and Vargas returned to Spain.

The loss of the 1622 treasure fleet was a disaster as Spain had already borrowed heavily to finance the war effort. It was vital that the *Atocha* and the *Santa Margarita* were found. In 1624, Nunez Melian was sent to salvage the treasure ships. In June 1626, a slave named Juan Banon spotted the wreck of the *Santa Margarita* and even managed to raise an ingot. Over the next four years, with the aid of a 680-pound copper diving bell, 380 silver ingots, 67,000 silver coins and eight bronze cannon were raised, though operations were hampered by bad weather and Dutch raiding parties. But there was still no sign of the *Atocha*.

When Melian was appointed governor of Venezuela, he hired Captain Juan de Anuez to take over the search, but his efforts were only sporadic and he came up with nothing. In 1641, Melian heard a rumour that some of the Indians who lived on the Keys knew where the *Atocha* lay and tried again. But he had found nothing by the time he died in 1644.

In 1715 and 1733, the Spanish lost entire fleets off the Florida coast. Again they tried to salvage them, though their efforts were harassed by the English colonists from Virginia and the Carolinas. Then, in 1819, the Spanish ceded Florida to the United States and gave up any hope of recovering their lost treasure fleets.

Modern-day treasure hunters had always assumed that the *Atocha* had gone down off Matecumbe Key and a number of searches were made there. But in 1970 a search of the Spanish salvage records in Seville revealed that she had sunk off Marquesas Key, eighty miles to the west.

American diver Mel Fisher had been keen to find the *Atocha* after his recovery of a thousand gold coins from the 1715 fleet gave him a taste for treasure hunting. He had already raised more than a

Mel Fisher and some of the Atocha*'s treasure*

Spanish galleon dismasted in a storm

million dollars' worth of treasure from the *Santa Margarita* and other ships when he started looking in earnest for the *Atocha*. His team got its first big break in 1973 when one of his sons found some gold, and later a silver bar, off Marquesas Key. Then in 1975, his eldest son Dirk found nine bronze cannon and they knew they were getting close.

Less than a week later, a boat sank suddenly on a calm sea, killing three divers – including Dirk Fisher and his wife. Despite this setback Mel Fisher continued to search for the *Atocha* for another ten years. Then on 20 July 1985, his team found her some thirty-five miles off Key West.

They brought up almost forty-seven tons of silver. There were silver bars and coins, mostly dating from the late 1500s to about 1620. The silver coins were *reales*, or 'pieces of eight' – one *real* was the pay a normal working man would receive in a month. They were also known as 'cob' coins, from the Spanish term *cobo de barra*, mean-

ing 'made from the bar'. Both the coins and the silver bars had a similar purity of around 92 to 98 per cent. Many of the coins were not even or round and in few was the stamp centred. This was because they were made by hand and struck purely for weight. Originally the coins had been stored in wooden boxes, but the wood had rotted away and the divers found the coins sitting there encrusted together in the shape of the box.

Over 150,000 gold coins and bars were also recovered. Gold is more resistant to underwater encrustation and the *Atocha's* gold could be seen gleaming on the sea floor throughout the wreck. The gold was 85 per cent pure, adulterated with 15 per cent silver. The gold coins came in different sizes, valued at one, two, four and eight escudos. A 'doubloon' comes for the word 'double' and originally applied to the common two-escudo coin. Later it came to mean any gold coin. Two silver pieces of eight equalled one escudo.

The doubloon carried the shield of the House of Habsburg on one side and the crusader's cross on the other, with a castle symbolising the kingdom of Castile and a lion symbolising the kingdom of Leon.

Hundreds of shaped and uncut emeralds were also found in the holds of the *Atocha*. They ranged in size from half a carat to over seventy-seven carats. One jewel alone was valued at over $2 million.

When Mel Fisher had raised it, both the State of Florida and the US government claimed they owned the treasure. After spending $10 million on finding the *Atocha*, Fisher spent a further $1.6 million on lawyers at over over two hundred judicial hearings. The case eventually ended up with the Supreme Court, who ruled that he did own the treasure. However, to preclude any further lawsuits, he agreed to donate 20 per cent of the *Atocha's* treasure, along with 20 per cent of anything else he might find, to a museum. The treasures of the *Atocha* are now on display in an old Key West naval station, now renamed the Mel Fisher Maritime Heritage Society Museum, which also houses a research and conservation laboratory, while his finds from the 1715 treasure fleet are on display at the Mel Fisher Center in Sebastian, Florida.

The *Lutine* is now principally known for her bell, which since 1986 has hung in the underwriting room of the Lloyd's building in London, its use largely confined to ceremonial occasions. HMS *Lutine* was originally *La Lutine* – 'the Sprite' – a French navy ship commissioned in 1785, four years before the French Revolution. On 18 December 1793, she was one of sixteen ships handed over to the British by French Royalists who wanted to keep them out of the hands of the republicans. Commissioned into the Royal Navy, she was stationed in the North Sea.

The silver coins from the *Santa Margarita* were reales: the 'pieces-of-eight' of pirate legend

On 9 October 1799, she left Great Yarmouth under the command of Captain Lancelot Skynner with 240 passengers and up to £2 million in coin and gold bullion. Some of the money was intended as pay for the British soldiers who were fighting in Holland; the rest to ease a cash crisis in Hamburg brought on by the Napoleonic Wars. According to a newspaper report, diamonds belonging with the Dutch crown jewels which had been sent to London for cleaning, were also on board. The cargo was insured by Lloyd's.

As the *Lutine* approached the Dutch coast, a gale blew up. Caught on a lee shore, she tried to reach shelter off the West Friesian Islands, but in the early hours of the following day she hit a sandbank off the island of Terschelling and sank. The British sloop *Arrow* and the corvette *Wolverine* rushed to her aid but they picked up one solitary survivor, some of the ship's equipment and a few corpses, including that of Captain Skynner. Local islanders collected another two hundred corpses, which they buried in a pit near Brandaris lighthouse.

As the *Lutine* lay in only three fathoms – eighteen feet of water – there was an immediate fear of looting, so the *Wolverine* moored over her. That winter was a bad one but, despite the weather, salvors managed to raise some cannon, then a chest containing Spanish *piastres*. In all they brought up fifty-eight gold bars, ninety-nine silver ones and 41,000 silver coins. But as the work went on they encountered a new problem. The packaging around the bullion began to disintegrate when touched and the divers were left groping for precious metal and coinage among the tangled rigging and smashed timbers of the ship.

In 1801, the Netherlands – then the Batavian Republic, a French protectorate – claimed the wreck and sold a salvage contract to a team of local divers. They had little luck: in that part of the

North Sea, the sandbanks' constant movement tends to bury anything on the sea floor. The hull had also moved and covered the place where the treasure had been found. However, local boats still made trips out to the wreck site on moonlit nights.

With the end of the Napoleonic Wars, the British put pressure on the new Dutch government who eventually agreed to allow Lloyd's to have half of any of the cargo raised. By that time, however, the wreck had been lost. It was found again in 1857 when a fisherman hauled in a buoy that had gone adrift and brought up with it a piece of the *Lutine*. Two silver spoons were raised, along with a quantity of *louis d'or*. The following year, more gold coins were found, along with gold and silver bars. Also in 1858, the rudder was raised, the wood of which was used to make tables and chairs for Lloyd's London headquarters. The raising of the rudder helped divers locate the stern of the

Traditionally the ringing of the Lutine Bell has marked the announcement of important news

ship, where the loot had been stored. This was now opened and more gold and silver was recovered. By the end of 1859, Lloyd's had received about £22,000 of an estimated £100,000 recovered to date. That means there should be another £1.9 million still lying on the seabed.

Dutch museums were full of relics from the *Lutine*, though little more bullion was raised. In 1862, one diver felt a hard surface with regular seams across it, like an array of ingots. But when he dived again, he found it was a floor buried under the sand. Further salvage attempts were made in 1907, 1910 and 1911, but the gold and silver coins and other relics brought up fetched no more than £135.

In 1938, the world's biggest dredger, the *Karimata*, was brought to the wreck site. A gold bar was brought up, followed by a coin dated 1797. But that was it – and it was even suggested that a diver had planted the gold bar.

The *Lutine's* bell was brought up on 17 July 1858 and eventually hung in the Royal Exchange building in Liverpool. The bell would be sounded when news of overdue ships was received: one stroke for bad news and two for good.

Had it been in place, the *Lutine* bell would certainly have sounded for HMS *Thetis*, a forty-six-gun frigate that sank on 5 December 1830. Putting out of Rio de Janeiro the day before with a cargo of gold and silver bars, plate and silver coin worth $810,000, she ran directly into the cliffs at Cape Frio at night under full sail. The current swept the ship away from the cliffs and she sank some 1,800 feet out to sea, drowning everyone on board. The wreck then broke up completely, scattering her treasure across the sea floor.

The possibility of salvaging her did not look too promising. She had sunk in deep water in an area known for its strong currents and frequent storms. But Captain Thomas Dickinson was determined to try. Armed with a diving bell made from a warship's iron water tank, and a pump to maintain pressure, he arrived off Cape Frio in January 1831.

He found what was left of the *Thetis* in a narrow cove in water thirty-five to seventy feet deep. Using explosives he blew out part of the northeast cliff to make a platform for a derrick 150 feet long which he made from the masts and spars of the *Thetis* that had washed ashore.

By late May, he had recovered nearly $13,000-worth of bullion. When a storm destroyed the derrick, he suspended a smaller diving bell from a cable strung between the cliffs and continued the hunt. Before he was recalled to England, he had recovered some $600,000. A further $148,000 was recovered after he left. But there is still $62,000-worth of gold and silver down there – that's $62,000 at 1830 prices.

In 1848, James Wilson Marshall, a carpenter from New Jersey, picked up a nugget of gold in the American River near a sawmill he was building, unwittingly sparking the California gold rush. The gold dug up in California had to be transported back to New York, and it is estimated that, between 1852 and her loss in 1857, around one third of the gold dug out of the hills in California – worth $150 million in 1850 prices – travelled on the SS *Central America*, operated by the United States Mail Steamship Company.

Although by this time there were several established overland routes between California and New York, the journey was a long and arduous one, not to mention one fraught with dangers; it was considered easier to transport the gold to the Pacific coast of Panama, cross the isthmus, and load it onto a ship in the Atlantic, from where it could be transported to New York.

On 2 September 1857, the SS *Central America* left Aspinwall – now Colón – in Panama, under the command of Captain William Lewis Herndon. She was carrying 476 passengers, 102 crew members, some 38,000 items of mail and over three tons of gold in ingots, coins, nuggets and dust mined from the western gold fields. The cargo included over 5,000 rare $20 'Double Eagle' gold pieces pressed from Californian gold in 1857 by the San Francisco Mint. Other coins and ingots were made privately by government-supervised assayers Blake & Co, Justh & Hunter, Harris, Marchand & Co, Wass Molitor & Co and Kellogg & Humbert, who made gold bricks weighing 933 troy ounces – almost eighty pounds!

On 10 September 1857, the *Central America* was hit by a hurricane off the coast of the Carolinas. The following day, at around 9 am, she sprang a leak. Finally, at about 8 pm on 12 September, the sea overcame her and she sank about 160 miles east of Cape Hatteras, North Carolina. There were three ships in the vicinity – the *El Dorado*, the *Ellen* and the *Marine*, who between them picked up some 160 survivors from the water. Captain Herndon went down with his ship and was acclaimed a hero for his composure in the face of adversity and his tireless efforts to save his passengers.

The *Central America* had taken twenty-one tons of gold with her to the bottom and the loss of such a valuable cargo sparked the 'Panic of 1857'. Unable to meet their payrolls or pay creditors, New York banks began to fail. Factories and stores began to close, touching off a financial crash in the US and Europe.

In 1985, a group of 161 investors based in Columbus, Ohio, raised more than $10 million to find the *Central America* and raise her cargo. The following year, after searching 1,400 square miles of the Atlantic Ocean, they located the ship's bell in 8,500 feet of water. In 1988, deep-sea diver Tommy Thompson recovered the treasure and numerous historic artefacts, using state-of-the-art technology he had developed. Court battles ensued but the Columbus group managed to hold on to 92 per cent of the find.

The *Lutine*'s bell, now in Lloyd's of London, weighs 106 pounds and measures 18 inches in diameter

Californian gold mined during the Gold Rush of the 1860s, and lost aboard the Central America.
The gold is a mixture of nuggets, coins, and ingots bearing the assayer's name stamp

More gold went down in 1922 when the P&O liner *Egypt* sank in the Bay of Biscay. She was an elegant 500-foot Edwardian passenger liner, displacing just under eight thousand tons. Her maiden voyage was to Bombay in September 1897. Most of her early days were spent on the Australian run, then from 1910 she cruised the Mediterranean and during World War I she saw service as a hospital ship.

On 19 May 1922, the *Egypt* left Tilbury bound for Bombay with some 355 passengers and crew aboard. She was also carrying five tons of gold ingots, ten tons of silver ingots and a large consignment of gold sovereigns, worth £1,083,527 – or £36 million at today's prices. Three days out, she was twenty-five miles off Ushant, when she encountered fog so dense that her captain was tempted to bring her to a halt. But as she was in a busy shipping lane, even that would not be safe, so she moved ahead slowly, sounding her whistle. But at 7 pm, off Cape Finisterre, she was rammed between the funnels by the *Seine*, a French cargo steamer which traded in the Baltic

and had had her bows strengthened to break ice. The *Egypt* heeled over from the impact and sank in twenty minutes with the loss of eighty-six lives.

The underwriters had to write off the cargo as she lay in over four hundred feet of water – twice the depth any diver had ventured at that time. Then the famous Italian salvage expert Giovanni Quaglia, founder of the *Società Ricuperi Marittimi*, or Sorima, took on the mission of recovering the bullion on behalf of Lloyd's insurers. In June he tried to locate the wreck using several novel methods – including employing a certain Father Innocent who claimed to be able to locate bullion using divining rods; bad weather, however, put paid to his efforts.

The following August, Quaglia employed the traditional method of towing a cable suspended between two vessels over the seabed to locate the wreck. She was lying upright on an even keel, but the strong room containing the bullion was a narrow chamber twenty-three feet long, three deck-levels down at the bottom of the ship.

Quaglia intended to get to it using an armoured

diving suit lowered to the wreck as an observation chamber. The diver would then use a phone link to direct operations carried out by a surface team using explosives and steel grabs lowered by cranes and winches from the salvage vessel *Artiglio* above.

It was slow work. At the height of the Depression Quaglia had to break off to raise more capital. The *Artiglio* was lost while trying to demolish the wreck of the American munitions ship *Florence H*, which had exploded and gone down in World War I off Quiberon, France. In May 1931, *Artiglio II* managed to blast away a portion of the *Egypt's* wreckage exposing the gold, but bad weather stopped them from attempting to recover it. Quaglia returned the following May and by June 1932, he had recovered £80,000.

When Quaglia arrived in London to visit Lloyd's, he was given a hero's welcome and newspapers ran the story around the world. He continued the search and by 1935 Quaglia had recovered some 95 per cent of the treasure. Seventeen gold bars, thirty silver ingots and 14,929 sovereigns remained unaccounted for, however, and they remain so today.

Mooring bollards located along the top port decking of the RMS Egypt *loom out of the blackness of the Bay of Biscay*

4 Lost Liners

In 1819, the paddle steamer *Savannah* crossed the Atlantic. Although she was the first steamship to do so, she was in fact fitted with sails, which she used most of the way. In 1831 the Canadian paddle steamer *Royal William* crossed the Atlantic under steam. But she had to stop every few days to have her boilers scraped and revert to sail. Then in 1838, the coastal steamer *Sirius* finally crossed the Atlantic using steam power alone.

Isambard Kingdom Brunel's *Great Western* was launched in April 1838 and was joined by a sister ship, the *Great Britain*, in 1845. With screw propulsion rather than a paddle wheel, and an iron hull, the *Great Western* was perhaps the first true ocean liner. But in 1846 she ran aground off the Irish coast. Her 180 passengers got ashore, but by the time she had been refloated almost a year later, her owners had gone bankrupt.

As liners established themselves as the way to cross the Atlantic in comfort and style, competition quickly developed between Samuel Cunard's 'Cunard Line' and the 'Dramatic Line' of Edward Knight Collins. While Cunard concentrated on safety and comfort, Collins went for speed and in 1850 the Dramatic Line's ship *Pacific* became the first ship to cross the Atlantic in under ten days. Things began to go wrong for Collins, however: on the *Atlantic's* maiden voyage to England, her paddle wheel was damaged by drift ice, and she developed engine trouble, but managed to limp safely into Liverpool.

In 1850 Collins launched the *Arctic*. Built for speed, she had a wooden hull, but no watertight compartments and few pumps. On 20 September 1854, she left Liverpool for New York under the command of Captain James Luce, carrying 153 crew members and 282 passengers, including the captain's young son, Collins's wife and their two children, Henry and Mary Ann, and five family members of Collins's partner, one James Brown.

As they approached the coast of North America on 27 September, they encountered fog. Luce, eager to make a quick passage to New York did not slow down but continued at thirteen knots, even though visibility was only half-a-mile. He did not even take the precaution of getting a crewman to sound a horn, warning of their approach.

At 12.15 pm, the *Arctic* crossed the path of the French steamer *Vesta*, under the command of Captain Alphonse Duchesne. The *Vesta's* iron hull struck the starboard of the *Arctic* tearing away ten feet of the bow and making three holes under the water line. The *Vesta* was damaged as well and lowered two lifeboats, one of which promptly capsized, drowning several passengers. Luce was convinced that the *Arctic* was relatively unharmed but when the second officer made an inspection of the hull, he found water pouring in.

To lighten the bow and lift it out of the water,

48

Luce had the anchor and anchor chain thrown overboard. The crew then tried to cover the holes in the side with sailcloth but this tore on jagged pieces of iron left by the *Vesta*. Luce now had a choice to make. He could either stay where he was and get help from the *Vesta* or make a run for the shore. As the *Vesta* itself seemed to be in trouble, he made a run for it. When the *Vesta's* lifeboat got in the way, he ran it down. The only survivor was Jassonet François, who grabbed a rope tossed to him by a passenger on the *Arctic* and was hauled on board.

The water was now pouring in through the *Arctic's* side quicker than the pumps could expel it, and the ship quickly filled with water. In less than two hours, the water put out the fires under the boilers, with the *Arctic* still thirty-five miles from shore. With no steam they were stranded. Luce gave the order to take to the boats – 'Women and children first'. But the stokers rebelled and rushed for the lifeboats, killing a crewman who got in the way.

The passengers began building rafts while apprentice engineer Stuart Holland fired a signal gun until the ammunition ran out in the hope of alerting nearby vessels. At 4.45 p.m, the *Arctic* sank. Captain Luce saw his son killed when the housing from the paddle wheel bobbed to the surface and crushed him. Luce clambered onto the paddle housing, while Jassonet François – who had survived two sinkings in one day – and others clung to any debris they found. That night, many of them perished in the cold Atlantic water. The following day, passing ships picked up a few survivors. Two lifeboats reached land, but another three that had been launched were never found. Of the 435 people on board the *Arctic*, only sixty-five survived. Among the dead were Mrs Collins and her two children.

The following day *Vesta* limped into port at St

John's, Newfoundland. Captain Duchesne was praised for his seamanship, while Luce shouldered the blame. He had been going too fast in the fog; he had then sailed away from the only ship in the vicinity that could have given him aid. Travelling at top speed had forced more water through the hole in the bow, hastening the *Arctic's* sinking. He had also failed to exercise proper discipline over the crew.

The sinking of the *Arctic* had some lessons for shipwrights too. It proved the superiority of iron hulls over wooden ones and hastened the introduction of watertight compartments.

Less than two years later, Collins's ship the *Pacific* disappeared with 150 passengers on a trip from Liverpool to New York in January 1856. No trace was found of her until a fisherman snagged his nets on a wreck in the Irish Sea between Anglesey and the Isle of Man in 1986. Meanwhile, Cunard had troubles of his own. That same month, the *Persia* ran into an iceberg, but she made it safely to New York. This stark contrast to Dramatic Line's safety record marked the end of the line for Collins. Passengers wanted safety not speed and the Dramatic Line folded in 1858.

The Quest for Speed

Fog banks are common off Nantucket. On 4 July 1898, the iron-hull *Cromartyshire* rammed the French liner *La Bourgogne* there. *La Bourgogne* sank with the loss of five hundred people. However, captains refused to heed the warnings. Double-hulled, watertight craft gave them the hubris to speed through patches of fog or ice to maintain schedules or set speed records.

The White Star Line's 15,400-ton *Republic* held the record between Boston and Queenstown (now Cóbh) County Cork. On 23 January 1909, she

> The water was now pouring in through the *Arctic's* side quicker than the pumps could expel it

The RMS Republic, *holed in her port side by the bows of the* Florida, *begins to founder*

steamed out of New York harbour with 742 passengers and crew on board, bound for the Mediterranean. Off Nantucket, she ran into fog, but her captain, William Sealby, only checked his speed slightly. The ship had a double bottom and a double layer of steel throughout. Sealby did take some cursory precautions, however, remaining on the bridge and ordering that the ship's whistle to be sounded at regular intervals.

Some miles to the east was the *Florida*, a small ship of the Lloyd Italiano Line carrying nine hundred immigrants to New York, many of them survivors of the earthquake that had destroyed Messina a month before. Her captain, twenty-nine-year-old Angelo Ruspini, was more cautious. He had slowed his ship, doubled the lookouts and, like Sealby, ordered the ship's whistle to be sounded regularly.

At 5.47 am, Sealby and the other officers on the bridge of the *Republic* heard a ship's whistle just off the port bow. He ordered the ship's engines

full astern. Turning hard to port, two whistle blasts were sounded to indicate that the ship was turning left: Sealby hoped the other vessel would do the same. Instead the *Florida* turned hard to starboard. There was a rumour that the helmsman had made a mistake and Ruspini was so angry that he hit him, although this was later denied by the crew. However, the *Florida* was now aimed directly at the *Republic*.

The officers on the bridge of the *Republic* saw the mast light of the *Florida* coming straight at them. Sealby ordered full speed ahead in an effort to get out of the way. But it was too late. The *Florida* hit her amidships, killing three passengers in their bunks. On the *Florida*, four crewmen were killed by the impact. For a moment, there seemed a danger that she might slice the *Republic* in two. But the *Florida's* poorly constructed bow crumpled. On deck, Mrs Filomena Cayliofera, a first-class passenger who was returning from visiting relatives in Italy, saw the *Florida* pull free from the *Republic* leaving her anchor stuck in a state-room. By the time Domini Roberto, another first-class passenger on the *Florida*, got on deck the *Republic* was just 'a faint blur in the darkness'.

On the *Republic*, the president of the Metropolitan Trust Company Brayton Ives saw several half-dressed passengers wandering about when a steward told him to put on his life jacket and directed him to the boat deck. Woken by the noise of the impact, Mr and Mrs Smallman tried to switch on the cabin light, but it would not work. Mrs Herbert L. Griggs found that her cabin ceiling had collapsed and she was also plunged into darkness.

As a safety feature, the *Republic* had been fitted with one of Marconi's new wireless telegraphy sets. The wireless operator, Jack Binns, awoke to find the radio room in ruins, with one wall and half the ceiling missing. Unable to telephone the bridge, he reported in person for instructions and was told to transmit a distress signal. The ship's electrical supply had failed, so Binns connected up a series of batteries and transmitted the British distress signal 'CQD', making the *Republic* the first ship to call for help by radio. His signal was picked up by the radio station at Siasconet, Nantucket. Binns told the Siasconet radio operator: '*Republic* rammed by unknown steamship. Twenty-six miles southwest of Nantucket lightship. Badly in need of immediate assistance.' She was already listing badly to port.

Within minutes, the radio operator A.H. Ginman rebroadcast the message. Captain Ransom of the *Republic's* sister ship *Baltic* acknowledged the call. Soon Cunard's *Lucania*, the French ship *La Touraine* and several other ships were on their way.

On deck, Sealby mustered the remaining 442 passengers and issued coffee and blankets. They remained calm. Agnes Shachilford was particularly sanguine as she had been shipwrecked twice before

'*Republic* rammed by unknown steamship. Twenty-six miles southwest of Nantucket lightship. Badly in need of immediate assistance.'

– once aboard a vessel that had run aground; the second when her ship had caught fire. Meanwhile, banging had been heard coming from Mrs Griggs's cabin. A hole was cut through the wall and she was then rescued. Mrs W.J. Mooney had also been pulled from her cabin by two seamen and carried on deck.

Below deck things were not so calm. As water poured through the side of the engine room, the stokers fled. Fortunately, Fourth Engineer Legg had the presence of mind to open the injector valves, which slowly introduced cold water and lowered the boiler pressure. (Boilers were liable to explode if suddenly dowsed with freezing seawater.)

On the *Florida*, where the bow had been crumpled for thirty feet, there was panic. Captain Ruspini quickly assured the passengers that the ship was not going to sink and had a sailcloth strung over the bow to block any leaks, a technique known as 'fothering'. He then circled back in search of the *Republic*. Guided by her foghorn, Ruspini pulled to within hailing distance and offered to take the *Republic's* passengers on board.

Sealby addressed his passengers, telling them that they were in no immediate danger but, to be on the safe side, they were going to be transferred to the *Florida*.

'I expect that you will be cool and not excited,' he said. 'Take your time in getting into the lifeboats. Remember, the women and children go first, and the first cabin next, and then the others. The crew will be the last to leave this vessel.'

Everyone did as they were told and remained calm, except for James B. Connolly, the author of a number of maritime books, who was upset that he could not bring his luggage. The transfer proved a long and difficult business, with the sea choppy and only ten lifeboats in use, but by 12.30,

A contemporary painting shows the passengers of the ill-fated Republic *being taken onto the* Baltic's *boats*

only a handful of the crew remained on the *Republic*. One of them was wireless-operator Binns who stuck at his post for fourteen hours, with only one meal break to swim over to the galley where he found some almonds and a few crackers. Outside his cabin he saw floating the mutilated bodies of a woman and man, later identified as Mrs Eugene Lynch and W.J. Mooney. The ship's doctor covered them with a blanket.

Between them, Binns and Ginman contacted seven ships in the area that steamed to the rescue. Binns signalled *La Touraine*: 'Ship's sinking, but will stick to the end.' This was overheard by the *Baltic's* wireless operator who radioed: 'Don't worry, old man, we are bursting our boilers to get to you.'

The *Baltic* reached the scene at midday on 24 January, but in the fog she could not see the stricken vessels. Her crew fired rockets, sounded foghorns and set off bombs in an effort to make contact. The *Baltic* had detonated its last bomb, when she received the message from Binns: 'You are right on course.'

Soon she was in hailing distance and it was decided to transfer the passengers off the *Republic* and the damaged and now dangerously overloaded *Florida* onto the *Baltic*. She was larger, far from full and had room for 1,600 extra passengers. This time the transfer did not go so smoothly, the Italian immigrants disagreeing with the notion that the first-class passengers should go first, and mutiny was threatened. As one of the *Republic's* officers later wrote, however: 'Discipline...was maintained and the privilege of class upheld.'

While the *Baltic* and the *Florida* made for New York, Sealby tried to salvage the *Republic*. She was taken in tow by the US destroyer *Seneca* and the coastguard cutter *Gresham*, with the *Furnessia* at the stern to act as a rudder. But she soon seemed certain to founder. Sealby and Second Officer Williams stayed on board to fire a blue flare when

'Don't worry, old man, we are bursting our boilers to get to you'

she was sinking as a signal for them to cut the cables.

At 6 pm, Williams found some cake and they had a last meal. Then at 8 pm they felt her going and tried to light the flare. But it was too wet to ignite, so Sealby fired his revolver in the air. As she sank by the stern they raced for the fore rigging and climbed as fast as they could, but Williams lost his grip and fell back on the railing. As the ship's stern hit the bottom – the *Republic* was 570 feet long and sank in 270 feet of water – there was a judder and a great roar. Williams released his hold on the railing and pitched into the water.

At 8.40 pm, nearly thirty-nine hours after she had been struck by the *Florida*, the *Republic* disappeared under the waves.

'When the water closed over the vessel,' said Williams, 'there seemed to be a great hole in the water, and there was a roar like thunder.'

Fearful of being sucked under, he swam as fast as he could. Eventually he came across a floating hatch-cover and tried to climb on to it, but it capsized, so he clung on to it. He had found another hatch-cover by the time a searchlight hit him. A lifeboat arrived and he was hauled aboard.

After Williams had fallen, Sealby had continued up the fore rigging. He was a hundred feet up when he tried again to light the flare. Still it would not ignite, so he fired the last round in his revolver. As the ship went down, Sealby found himself in a whirlpool, but air trapped beneath his greatcoat kept him afloat. Eventually, it soaked through and began to drag him down. He could not get it off, but was saved when a table floated by. Numb from the cold, he clung on to the table while he reloaded his revolver and fired two shots. Soon after the lifeboat carrying Williams arrived. The rowers spotted Sealby waving a towel and hauled him aboard. Ruing the demise of the *Republic*, Sealby told Williams: 'Game to the last, she went down with flying colours.'

Meanwhile on board the *Baltic*, James B. Connolly was still complaining about his luggage and the general unhelpfulness and incompetence of the crews of both the *Republic* and the *Baltic*, and a fight nearly broke out when the ship's barber accused him of being a coward. The barber and the *Republic's* chef later signed an affidavit, saying that they had seen Connolly trying to push in front of the women and children when the passengers were being transferred from the *Florida* to the *Baltic*, an accusation Connolly vehemently denied.

In New York, the *Baltic* was greeted with excitement and Jack Binns was accorded short-lived celebrity status on both sides of the Atlantic. When the *Florida* arrived in port, Captain Ruspini was greeted with a kiss from the Italian consul general and a band playing 'Hail the Conquering Hero'.

The *Empress of Ireland*

Fog was also the cause of the loss of the 14,191-ton *Empress of Ireland*, bound from Quebec City to Liverpool on 29 May 1914. On board were the actor Laurence Irving, son of the legendary Henry Irving, and his wife, the actress Mabel Hackney, returning from a successful tour of Canada, and 170 members of the Salvation Army on their way to a convention in London. At around 2 am, they were asleep and the *Empress of Ireland* was just east of Rimouski, where the St Lawrence River opens out into the sea. Some eight miles distant, Captain Henry Kendall spotted the approaching mast lights of the Norwegian collier *Storstad*. The *Empress of Ireland* was still close to shore, having just dropped her pilot at Father Point. The *Storstad* was also hugging the coast as she was about to pick up her pilot for the journey up river to Montreal. Captain Kendall judged that he could cross the *Storstad's* path, then set a course for open water. As soon as he completed this manoeuvre the fog rolled in, engulfing first the *Storstad* then the *Empress of Ireland*.

If Kendall had continued on his new course the two ships would have passed each other. But Kendall was a cautious man. Once in the fog bank, he ordered all engines to be thrown into reverse, slowing the ship. He sounded the ship's horn three times warning other traffic of his presence and the *Empress of Ireland* and the *Storstad* exchanged warning signals in the fog.

But the *Storstad* had changed course too. The captain was asleep in his cabin, but the first mate on the bridge had seen the *Empress of Ireland's* red port navigational lamp before the fog closed in. Assuming the *Empress of Ireland* to be on his port side, he turned to starboard, bringing her onto a collision course.

Suddenly through the fog Captain Kendall saw the lights of the *Storstad* reappear. They were less than ten yards away. Using a megaphone, he shouted to the commander of the *Storstad* to throw his engines into reverse while he turned hard to starboard to minimise the impact.

The *Storstad* was still travelling at around ten knots when she struck the *Empress of Ireland* on her starboard side between her two chimneys. Her bow sliced through the liner's steel ribs like a knife. The *Storstad* was fully loaded and her longitudinal bracing had been strengthened for icebreaking. Her bow smashed into the *Empress of Ireland* to a depth of twenty-five feet, leaving a gaping hole fourteen feet wide. The *Empress of Ireland* immediately began to go down. Despite the rule that portholes were supposed to be closed once the ship was underway, some had been left open. There was no time to close the watertight doors, and water poured in so fast that people sleeping in the starboard cabins stood no chance of escape.

As the ship began listing heavily, Captain Kendall ordered full speed ahead and turned for the shore in an attempt to run the *Empress* aground. But the engines chose this moment to break down. Suddenly all the lights went out. Five or six lifeboats were launched successfully and those who could find their way to the side in the

The Empress of Ireland *sinks in the North Atlantic, 29 May 1914, just two years after the loss of the* Titanic.
More passengers would lose their lives in the Empress *tragedy than went down with the more famous* Titanic

darkness threw themselves into the freezing water.

Ten minutes later the liner was lying on her side with hundreds of people clinging to her hull. Fourteen minutes after the collision, the *Empress of Ireland* sank completely. By that time the last frozen survivor had been fished from the water. Of the 1,477 on board, 1,012 lost their lives, including 840 passengers – eight more passengers had died than in the *Titanic* disaster.

Captain Kendall was one of the survivors. He had been thrown from the bridge by the impact and was fished from the water by the *Storstad*. As soon as he got on board he said to the *Storstad's* captain: 'You sunk my ship.' However, a crewman later testified that there was a serious fault with the *Empress of Ireland's* steering that caused her to wobble on her course.

The wreck sits in 130 feet of water. In the summer of 1914, a salvage company blew a hole in her side to retrieve the first-class mail, the purser's safe and $150,000 in silver bullion – worth more than $2 million today. More recently divers found a box of newspapers, dated 27 May 1914, the day before the *Empress of Ireland* sailed.

Sister Ships of the *Titanic*

In the 1880s, German liners began to outstrip the British in speed and comfort, but Thomas Ismay, the founder of the White Star Line, was determined to fight back and, in 1889, brought the *Oceanic* into service. She had luxury cabins with private bathrooms equipped with fresh-water taps and electric bells to summon the stewards. Ismay died in 1900 and the White Star Line was taken over by his son Bruce, who continued the struggle for the control of the North Atlantic. With William James Pirrie of the Belfast shipbuilder Harland & Wolff, he set about building a new generation of luxury liners. The keel of the *Olympic* was laid down in December 1908 and three months later work started on the *Titanic*.

The 45,324-ton *Olympic* made her maiden voyage to New York on 14 June 1911. The only complaint about her, it seemed, was the lack of cigar holders in the first-class washrooms. On 20 September, she slipped out of the Solent on her fifth voyage to New York. As she rounded Eagle Point on the Isle of Wight, she ran alongside the 7,350-ton cruiser, HMS *Hawke*. Hydrodynamic pressure sucked the *Hawke* towards the *Olympic* and the two ships collided. The *Hawke's* bow was badly damaged and only hastily rigged collision pads prevented her sinking. The collision also ripped two holes in the side of the *Olympic* and damaged one of her propellers. No one was killed, but the passengers were taken off by tender and the *Olympic* returned to Southampton for repairs, while the *Hawke* limped into Portsmouth. The captain of the *Olympic* was exonerated. But this accident did not augur well. The captain's name was Edward J. Smith – known to customers of the White Star Line as the 'millionaire's captain'. Smith it was who would be chosen for the White Star Line's ultimate post: commanding the *Titanic* on her maiden voyage (*see Chapter 10*).

Following the *Titanic's* disastrous first – and last – voyage, the first International Convention for Safety of Life at Sea was called in London. Under its rules, all ships had to carry enough lifeboats for all those on board. Ships had to maintain a twenty-four-hour radio watch and a joint UK-US International Ice Patrol was set up to warn of icebergs in the North Atlantic shipping lanes.

After the sinking of the *Titanic*, the *Olympic* was withdrawn from service for six months so that her double bottom could be extended up the sides of the ship and the bulkheads separating the watertight compartments could be raised to the level of the bridge deck. An additional forty-eight lifeboats were installed, bringing the total to sixty-eight. However, these did not save the lives of seven men aboard the Nantucket lightship that the *Olympic* sliced through and sank in foggy weather in 1934. The *Titanic's* sister ship *Britannic* was to have been even more luxurious than her illustrious predecessor, but before she could enter commercial service with the White Star Line, the First World War had broken out and she was handed over to the Admiralty, who fitted her out as a hospital ship. She saw service in the Mediterranean. After delivering a shipload of patients – some three thousand – to Southampton, on 12 November 1916, she set sail again. After taking on coal in Naples, she was steaming through the Kea Channel, between the Greek mainland and the island of Kea just east of Athens, on the morning of 20 November 1916, when at 8 am she was shaken by an explosion.

On the bridge was Captain Charles Bartlett, a White Star veteran known as 'Iceberg Charlie' because of his ability to 'smell' ice. Unfortunately, he had no such ability when it came to mines. One had exploded on the *Britannic's* starboard bow in just about the same place the *Titanic* had been holed. Since the sinking of the *Titanic*, her sister ships had been fitted with a pneumatic tube that connected the bridge and the radio room. Bartlett used this to order the wireless operator to send out a distress signal. He also ordered the lifeboats to be uncovered and the watertight doors to be

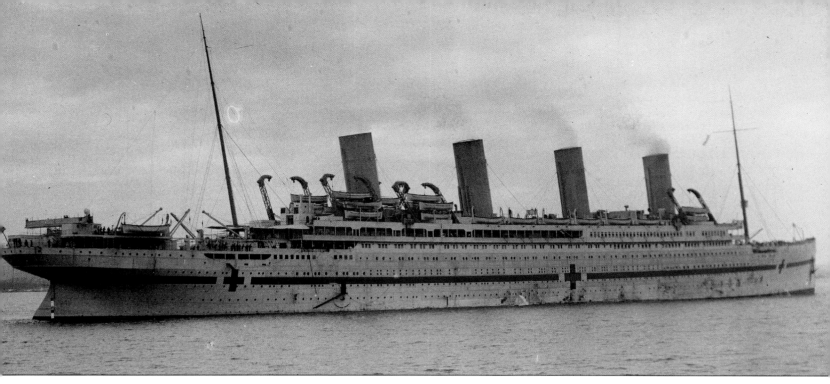

RMS Britannic, *seen here in her hospital ship livery, would suffer the same fate as her ill-fated sister ship, the* Titanic

closed. But the doors to boiler rooms five and six would not close and they flooded, filling six forward compartments with water. The ship could still float with six watertight compartments flooded, but this was the maximum number that could flood if the ship was to survive.

Even though they were in a war zone, some of the portholes had been left open. As the *Britannic* began to list to starboard, the portholes on E and F decks went under. Water flooded the decks. Realising that his ship was going to sink, Captain Bartlett made a dash for the island of Kea, hoping to ground her in the shallows. But this only drove more water into the ship, so Bartlett ordered the engines to stop.

Before the engines were shut down, two lifeboats had been lowered prematurely on the port side. They were smashed by the turning propeller which by then was clear of the water. Most of those on board were killed. One lucky survivor was Nurse Violet Jessop. She had been a stewardess on the *Olympic* when it had collided with the *Hawke*. The following year, she had sailed on the *Titanic*. This time, she had jumped clear just before the propeller hit the lifeboat, but was drawn down in its suction. Struggling to the surface, she hit her head on the bottom of the wrecked lifeboat, fracturing her skull. She was going down again when someone from the other lifeboat grabbed her and pulled her on board.

Captain Bartlett gave the order to abandon ship, directing the evacuation from the bridge with a megaphone. When everyone else was safely away, he gave one last blast on the ship's whistle and stepped into the sea. He watched from a collapsible dinghy as the water lapped up her decks. Then the boilers exploded and the *Britannic* disappeared under 395 feet of water.

The *Britannic* had taken fifty-five minutes to sink. The Royal Navy and Greek fishing boats were soon on hand to pick up the survivors. Of the over one thousand on board, only thirty died. Had the ship been sunk on the homeward journey when she was full of wounded soldiers the death toll would have been enormous.

The court of enquiry agreed with Captain Bartlett that the *Britannic* had probably been sunk by a mine, as no torpedo track had been seen. Jacques Cousteau dived on the wreck in 1976 and naval disaster expert Dr Robert Ballard examined it in 1995, but neither came up with anything to explain why the *Britannic* went down so much faster than the *Titanic*.

The Mystery of the *Morro Castle*

There is also a mystery surrounding the sinking of 11,520-ton liner *Morro Castle*. Named for the fortress that overlooks Havana Bay, she plied between New York and Havana for the Ward Line. It was known that there was discontent on board. The crew was demanding more pay and better food, but the anti-union management was unsympathetic. Captain Robert Wilmott accused junior radio operator and union organiser George Alagna of being a communist. It is also known that Wilmott lived in fear of the chief radioman, the six-foot-two George Rogers.

To supplement their meagre wages, crewmen smuggled illegal aliens, narcotics and rum from Cuba. Captain Robert Wilmott conducted regular searches of the crew's quarters for contraband. Cases of Cuban rum were thrown overboard in full view of the crew. Gambling was also rife and Wilmott threw a roulette wheel and other gaming equipment over the side. But he could not stop his men drinking and gambling on shore with the passengers on their last night in Havana before setting sail on 7 September 1934. They were returning to the US where Prohibition had only just been repealed and some states still banned alcohol.

On the evening of 8 September, the *Morro Castle* was six miles off the coast at Atlantic City, New Jersey, when Captain Robert Wilmott died of a suspected heart attack in his bathtub. Command passed to First Officer William Warms. There was a storm and the *Morro Castle* was making just eight knots as waves broke over her bow.

At about 2.45 am, a fire broke out in a locker on the promenade deck. The flames spread quickly. Warms attempted to manoeuvre the ship so that the wind would blow the fire to the stern, but he refused to send out an SOS, to save the company the expense of a salvage fee. By this time the ship was engulfed in smoke. Some of the passengers who had retired to their cabins early and dead drunk, burnt to death.

Warms was determined to make it to New York, forty miles away, while a junior officer named Hansen said their only chance was to beach on the New Jersey coast. A fight broke out.

Acting on their own initiative, Rogers and Alagna decided to send out a distress signal before the fire spread to the wireless room. The SOS went out at 3.24 am and several ships responded.

Seven minutes later, the ship lost all power. The anchor was dropped and the order was given to abandon ship. The crew raced for the lifeboats to save themselves. One lifeboat reached shore with thirty-one crew members on board and only one passenger. Another, carrying nineteen crew members and one passenger, reached the sandy beaches of Atlantic City.

At about dawn those left on board began to leap from the burning ship. Some of the hardier passengers managed to swim ashore. Seventy-one people were taken aboard *Monarch of Bermuda*, twenty-one aboard *Andrea S. Luckenbach*, sixty-five aboard *City of Savannah*, and sixty-seven aboard *Paramount*, a local fishing boat. Later that day, the gutted hulk of the *Morro Castle* drifted ashore.

In total, 137 were lost, most of them passengers. Warms and four other officers were charged with negligence. He was found guilty and sentenced to two years in jail. The chief engineer, Eban S. Abbott, who had ordered his men to stay below then ran for the lifeboats himself, was sentenced to four years. These sentences were reversed by higher courts, and no one served a day in jail for the disaster.

> The crew raced for the lifeboats to save themselves. One lifeboat reached shore with thirty-one crew members on board but with only one passenger

58

Suspicion would later fall on George Rogers. Although he was hailed as a hero for staying at his post and sending out the distress signal, it appears he had a long criminal record. It is thought that he may have poisoned Wilmott and started the fire to cover up his crime. He was subsequently involved in a series of murders and went back to prison.

In an effort to shake the negative publicity, the Ward Line was renamed the Cuba Mail Line. Congressional hearings following the wake of the disaster led to the adoption of more stringent safety regulations and the US belatedly joined the International Convention for the Safety of Life at Sea (SOLAS), first convened in 1914.

Another victim of fire was the luxury liner *Normandie*. When she was launched in 1935, she was the heaviest ship ever built, displacing 79,280 tons. And at 1,029 feet, she was the first liner over a thousand feet long. On her maiden voyage to New York, she won the Blue Riband for the fastest crossing and set a world speed record, covering 744 nautical miles in a single day at an average speed of just under thirty knots. When she arrived in New York, she had gone so fast that all the paint had been stripped from the lower part of her bow.

After the US entered the war in December 1941, the *Normandie* was requisitioned by the government and converted into a troop ship. Her fittings were removed and stored in a New York warehouse. In the early afternoon of 9 February 1942, workmen were removing an ornamental fountain when sparks from a welding torch set fire to a pile of life jackets. Much of the interior had already been stripped and no one could find the fire alarm which, in any case, had been disconnected. The nearest fire hose was hidden under other equipment, but when it was located it rendered only a dribble of water. The ship's own onboard fire station had no phone, and the

When the *Normandie* was launched in 1935, she was the heaviest ship ever built, displacing 79,280 tons

Normandie's direct line to the New York Fire Department had also been cut. Consequently it took the NYFD twelve minutes to arrive, by which time the interior was an inferno and a pall of smoke extended over New York City and Nassau County.

The ship was quickly evacuated. At the time she had caught fire, there had been three thousand people on board, more than she would have been carrying on a transatlantic voyage. Ninety-three people were injured and two died. Meanwhile, fireboats dowsed the *Normandie* with thousands of gallons of water. By 6 pm, the fire was out. But so much water had been pumped on board that she was top-heavy and began to list to port, away from the pier.

New York Mayor Fiorello LaGuardia rushed to the scene and told the press: 'Everything is all right now.' He was wrong. The ship's designer, Russian émigré Vladimir Yourkevitch, urged the US navy to open the seacocks, so that she would settle upright on the bottom. They would not listen and, that night, she rolled over on her side.

Her loss was a huge blow to morale. There were rumours that there had been sabotage and six separate enquiries attempted to find who was to blame. Meanwhile the superstructure was cut away. On 4 August 1943, pumps began emptying water from the hull. By 10 August, she had reached forty-five degrees, but it took until 27 October to right her completely. She was then towed to the Brooklyn navy yard where there was still some hope of turning her into a troopship. But the government changed its mind and she was sold as scrap to a firm in New Jersey, where she was finally raised from the water on 6 October 1947. However, much of the fine artwork taken from her interior before the fire can now be found adorning restaurants, hotels and other prestigious buildings around New York and in Florida.

The Wilhelm Gustloff, *originally intended to be named the* Adolf Hitler, *in her incarnation as a cruise liner*

The Greatest Maritime Disaster: the Tragedy of the *Wilhelm Gustloff*

The greatest ever sea disaster, in terms of loss of life, occurred in the Baltic on the bitterly cold night of 30 January 1945. That day the former cruise liner *Wilhelm Gustloff*, which had spent the war serving as a troopship, hospital ship and barracks for the German navy, left the Baltic port of Gotenhafen – now Gdynia in Poland. The advancing Soviet army had already broken through and had reached the Gulf of Danzig (now Gdansk), cutting off the Germans in what had been East Prussia: the only way out was by sea.

The 26,000-ton *Wilhelm Gustloff* was to have been named the *Adolf Hitler*, but at the last moment she was given the name of the head of the Swiss Nazi Party who had been assassinated by a Jewish student in 1936. She was designed to carry a maximum of 1,865 people, but that night when she pulled out of port she was carrying 10,582 refugees, including women, children and the elderly, and soldiers and sailors, many of whom were sick or wounded. The last to board were the mayor of Gotenhafen and his family. They were given the suite of cabins reserved exclusively for Hitler, who had never set foot on the ship and by then seemed unlikely to have the opportunity to do so.

When the *Gustloff* left Gotenhafen, the weather was poor. It was snowing and the wind was gusting up to force seven. It was ten degrees below zero and there were ice floes in the water. She had no escort and her only protection was a few anti-aircraft guns. In the choppy seas she could only make twelve knots, and Captain Petersen could not zigzag as the lane swept clear of mines was too narrow and, as they were also in danger of air attack if the weather cleared, he thought it best to make a dash for it at night.

Petersen also ordered that the ship be illuminated, considering collision with other craft in the low visibility a greater danger than with submarines. There was some justification for thinking this, as German minefields had kept the Soviet Baltic fleet bottled up at Kronstadt for most of the war. But the recent armistice between the Soviet Union and Finland allowed the Russians to operate from Finnish territory.

The 780-ton Soviet submarine *S-13*, commanded by Captain Alexander Marinesko, was now patrolling the Baltic. But in nineteen days at sea he had only come across small civilian craft in the waters of Lithuania. He was looking for naval transport evacuating troops to the west, but found none along the coastline where he expected them.

At 8.35 pm, he surfaced. Duty officer Lieutenant Yuri Yefremenko climbed into the conning tower. He saw a light which he first took to be the lighthouse at the end of the Hela peninsula. Marinesko took a look and decided it was too far north and that it had to be a ship. Yefremenko was sent below to plan the attack. The men went to battle stations. The submarine turned towards the light and Marinesko ordered full steam ahead.

Petersen was still oblivious to the danger. He may have been a little overconfident because, even though the ship was massively overcrowded, he had

enough life-saving equipment for everyone on board. But the lifeboats had not been swung out of their davits and no one had checked to see if they were free of ice.

Marinesko figured that his quarry might be under the protection of a destroyer, so he decided to make his move from the coastal side, even though there was a greater danger of mines there, or running aground in the shallows. He closed to a thousand metres, ordered the torpedoes to be set to run at a depth of three metres, then fired three at three-second intervals.

At 9.08 pm, all three torpedoes hit the *Gustloff*. The first hit below the helm; the second exploded under the swimming pools; the third hit amidships, destroying the engine room. The *Gustloff* listed to starboard, righted itself, and then listed to port. She launched distress rockets and sent an SOS.

Unable to contact the engine room, Petersen gave the order to abandon ship, but she was already listing so far to port that the starboard lifeboats could not be lowered. Several became overloaded. A cable snapped sending dozens of

The Wilhelm Gustloff *as she is today, as seen by diver Mike Boring. The name can be seen along the bow*

people splashing into the freezing water sixty feet below. Other lifeboats cast off with only a few passengers on board. Many passengers arrived on deck without lifejackets and few had any idea of the drill. There was little supervision. One deck officer who was supposed to be supervising the loading simply took a place in the lifeboat for himself.

Quickly the *Gustloff* began to sink at the bow. In less than fifty minutes, she had sunk beneath the icy black waters of the Baltic, taking with her 9,343 men, women and children. It was impossible to survive for more than a matter of minutes in the freezing water but, astonishingly, 1,239 people were saved by German ships in the area. One escort vessel had managed to get alongside in fifteen minutes, but most of the people they hauled out of the water were already dead.

One woman had survived the freezing temperatures thanks to her expensive fur coat. But it had been made slippery by the sea water, and she continually slipped through the hands of her would-be rescuers and was last seen drifting away in the darkness.

When the heavy cruiser *Admiral Hipper*, which already had 1,500 refugees on board, arrived, the passengers still on board the *Gustloff* cheered. But while her captain was trying to figure out how to take them off, torpedo tracks were spotted and she made off, leaving the *Gustloff* to her fate.

The broken wreck of the *Wilhelm Gustloff* is a designated grave site and is normally off-limits to divers and salvage crews. However, in May 2003 a team of British and American divers led by Mike Boring was allowed to survey her.

The *Andrea Doria*

The notorious fog off Nantucket was to claim another victim, on 26 July 1956. At 11 pm on 26 July 1956 the Swedish cruise ship *Stockholm* ran into the side of the Italian passenger ship *Andrea Doria*. Although both ships were equipped with

radar, officers made miscalculations in low visibility and the two ships were travelling at full speed when they collided.

The 697-foot *Andrea Doria* was the first ocean liner to have three swimming pools. She also had two sets of radar, which were by then standard equipment in the merchant marine. She was on her way from Genoa and was scheduled to arrive in New York harbour the following morning, a schedule Captain Piero Calamai, a veteran of thirty-nine years at sea, wanted to keep. So even though, at times, the bow was invisible from the bridge, Captain Calamai reduced speed only a little; he did, however post a lookout in the bows and ordered the watertight doors closed.

The *Andrea Doria's* radar picked up the *Stockholm* at 10.45 pm. She was seventeen nautical miles away, just four degrees off the starboard bow – that is, almost dead ahead. But she seemed to be turning to port. Assuming that she was a small coastal vessel which would head north to Nantucket, Captain Calamai decided to pass the oncoming ship starboard side to starboard side, rather than port side to port side which is the normal rule of the sea. At 11.05 pm, Calamai ordered the helm four degrees to port to give the oncoming ship a wider berth.

But on board the *Stockholm*, radar indicated that the *Andrea Doria* was on her port side, rather than on the starboard. The *Stockholm* had no plans to turn north to Nantucket and Third Officer Carstens-Johannsen, who was in command, expected to pass port side to port side. When the two ships' navigation lights came within visual range at about two miles distant, they were at such a slight angle that the *Stockholm* saw the *Andrea Doria* to her port, while the *Andrea Doria* saw the *Stockholm* to her starboard. Carstens-Johannsen now turned to starboard to increase the distance been the two ships as they passed. In fact, he was turning directly into the path of the *Andrea Doria*.

Only a mile away by then, Captain Calamai could not believe his eyes. The oncoming ship was turning directly across his bows. He ordered the helm hard to port. At the critical moment, Carstens-Johannsen had been called to the ship's phone. It was the lookout in the crow's nest telling him that he could see a ship's lights twenty degrees to port. It was only when he took a look for himself that he grasped the situation. He ordered the helm hard to starboard and the engines full astern.

At 11.10 pm, the icebreaking bow of the Swedish ship struck the Italian liner broadside. One of the survivors recalled seeing a large shower of sparks and hearing the crash of metal as the *Stockholm* slammed into the starboard side of the *Andrea Doria*, ripping open seven of her eleven decks with a gash that cut her almost to the keel. She immediately began to list. The *Stockholm* reversed her engines to pull her bow out of the liner's side, but as she pulled free she bumped along the side of the *Andrea Doria*, making several more holes.

In cabin fifty-six, Thure Peterson saw the bow of the *Stockholm* appear through the bulkhead before he passed out. In cabin fifty-two, a young girl was killed instantly while her sister, Linda Morgan, was flung out of bed by the impact and eventually reunited with her mother who was trapped in cabin fifty-four. The wife of the mayor of Philadelphia, Mrs Richardson Dilworth, who had recently read the book *A Night to Remember*, awoke to find her husband on the floor.

'I think we've hit an iceberg like the *Titanic*,' she said.

Like the *Titanic*, the *Andrea Doria* was thought to be unsinkable. Built with the most modern technology available, she had all the newest safety equipment. Just three years old, she had crossed the Atlantic a hundred times. But even before she was holed, the *Andrea Doria* was already unstable, her nearly empty fuel tanks making her top heavy.

In cabin fifty-six of the *Andrea Doria*, Thure Peterson saw the bow of the *Stockholm* appear through the bulkhead before he passed out

One of her fuel tanks was holed and, as water poured in one side, the remaining fuel poured out of the other, increasing the list. It soon became clear that the Italian ship was doomed.

The list was soon so bad that most of the lifeboats were useless. Those along the port side lay against the side of the ship and could not be lowered, while those on the starboard swung out too far for the passengers to get into them. Even if the starboard lifeboats could have been lowered fully laden, they could only carry 1,004 of the 1,706 on aboard. So Captain Calamai did not issue the order to abandon ship for fear of panicking the passengers.

Eventually the starboard lifeboats were lowered and ropes were rigged to lower passengers into them. The first got away an hour after the collision, carrying with them some of the crew. The *Stockholm* also sent boats. But first-class passengers had to wait at their muster station for three hours without instructions of what to do and the tourist-class passengers, deep in the belly of the ship, had to fight their way up the companionways as waves cascaded down on them. In some cases, this took ninety minutes. And in the confusion, a pregnant woman jumped into the water to save her children.

An SOS brought a flotilla of rescue ships led by the French liner *Ile de France*, which was over two hours away. When she arrived she picked up 753 survivors in lifeboats. Other ships soon arrived to pick up more survivors. In all, forty-six people died, while 1,660 were rescued.

When evacuation had been completed, Captain Calamai stayed on board, thinking he was the only one left. In fact, there was a third-class passenger in the hospital who had slept through the whole thing. He was later evacuated. Although it was clear that the *Andrea Doria* was going to sink, Calamai still thought there was a chance of towing

Like the Titanic *before her, the* Andrea Doria *was popularly believed to be unsinkable. Like the* Titanic, *she was not*

her to shallow water. But when no tug arrived, at 5.30 am he stepped on board a lifeboat.

After struggling to stay afloat for eleven hours, the crippled Italian liner sank at 10.09 am on 29 July. The badly damaged *Stockholm* was towed into New York harbour two days later. The *Andrea Doria* was left where she lay, 225 feet down. A yellow buoy marks the wreck and she became a popular site for diving. She lies on her starboard side. A hole has been cut in her port side to retrieve the ship's safe. And, on a clear day, the name on her side can still be seen.

The *Queen Elizabeth*

The last of the great liners of the golden age to succumb to fire was the *Queen Elizabeth*. Due to be launched as a cruise liner in 1938, the build-up to the Second World War delayed her completion, and in 1940, she was converted into a troopship; her maiden voyage as a passenger ship was delayed

until 1946. She made her final Atlantic crossing on 5 November 1968. Then she was sold to a group of Philadelphia businessmen for £3.25 million and sailed to Port Everglades where she opened as a tourist attraction in February 1969. By the end of the year she had been closed down by the local authorities as a fire hazard and was losing money.

In February 1971 she was taken to Hong Kong where she was to become a floating university. Renamed *Seawise University* she anchored off Tsing Yi Island near Kowloon. By January 1972, her £5-million refit was almost complete. But security on board was lax. On 9 January an arsonist set her ablaze. The fire could not be controlled. Eventually she capsized and the hulk, now on its side, continued to burn for over a week. The bulk of the wreck that appeared above the water was cut down for scrap. Eventually the remaining underwater portion, deemed a hazard to navigation, was removed and used as landfill for one of the runways of the new Hong Kong Airport.

The Andrea Doria *on her way to the bottom of the sea. Fortunately, most passengers and crew survived the ordeal*

5 Supertankers

On Sunday 19 March 1967 an oil tanker named the *Torrey Canyon* ran aground on the Seven Stones reef that lies to the northeast of the Scilly Isles. She was carrying 120,000 tons of crude oil from Kuwait. This was the world's first major oil tanker disaster. It would not be the last.

At 974 feet long, the *Torrey Canyon* was one of the largest ships afloat in 1967. She had started life at 810 feet but had been 'jumbo-ed' by Sasebo Heavy Industries in Japan during the oil boom of the 1960s, nearly doubling her capacity. The property of a US company based in Bermuda, she sailed under the Liberian flag with an Italian crew, but at the time of the accident she was working for BP, carrying oil from the Persian Gulf to Milford Haven in Wales.

In command was Captain Pastrengo Rugiati, who had been born on Elba and trained in the Merchant Navy Academy in Livorno. An experienced officer, he had served as a ship's master since 1952 and had been captain of the *Torrey Canyon* since March 1966. His wife was ill and it had been more than a year since his last holiday. To add to the stress, he did not get on with his chief officer.

Too big to go through the Suez Canal, the *Torrey Canyon* had made her way around the Cape of Good Hope. On the afternoon of 14 March, she had passed between the island of Tenerife and Gran Canaria, from where Captain Rugiati called the ship's agent in Milford Haven, who informed him that if he did not arrive by the high tide at 11 pm on 18 March, he would not be able to enter port until the 24th. In the meantime the neap tide meant the water would not be high enough for his huge ship to get into harbour. This worried Rugiati. Even to get into the harbour on the 18th, he would have to move some of the oil from the tanks amidships and pump it into tanks fore and aft (When fully laden, tankers tend to sag in the middle, increasing their draught). This process would take about five hours and needed to be done in calm waters to avoid the spillage which could be caused by any rolling.

The *Torrey Canyon* had two 25,290-horsepower steam turbines, driving a single propeller and giving her a top speed of sixteen knots. At that speed, the earliest Rugieri could expect to arrive at Milford Haven was 5 pm. There was no time to be wasted. His employers would not be pleased if he had to sit off Milford Haven for five days. A relief crew was waiting which would have to be put up in expensive hotels, and the crewmen on board would not be pleased at having their leave delayed either.

Rugiati set a course of 018 degrees from the Canaries. This should have taken the *Torrey Canyon* five miles to the west of the Isles of Scilly. The ship was put on autopilot. At noon on 17 March, he checked his position and found that he

The Torrey Canyon *spilled hundreds of tons of oil into the English Channel*

However, 018 degrees did put them rather close to the Seven Stones reef that lay to the northwest of the Scillies. At the time the *Torrey Canyon* would pass it, they would be covered by the high tide and invisible.

At 7 am, Rugiati arrived on the bridge. His aim was to alter course to 325 degrees roughly halfway from the Scillies to the Seven Stones reef, taking the *Torrey Canyon* through the deep water channel between them. Then he would go back to 018 degrees. But when he came to the point where he wanted to make the turn, he found some fishing boats in the way, so he had to delay the course alteration. When he came to make the turn, he left the autopilot engaged. With it on he could only alter his course by three degrees. So he made one alteration of three degrees, and a second of two degrees, giving him a heading of 013.

During the night the strong north-easterly current between Ushant and the Scillies – a common occurrence – had pushed the ship to the east, which is why the Scillies appeared on the port side rather than the starboard. It had also pushed the ship to the north, nearer to the Seven Stones reef. This problem was compounded by sightings taken by the officer of the watch. He had mistaken the landmarks he had seen as putting the ship much more southerly than she actually was.

At 8.42, Rugiati switched off the autopilot, brought the ship around to 000 degrees, then switched the autopilot back on. At 8.48, the officer of the watch took another reading. This time he could clearly see the Seven Stones lightship. When he plotted his position, he found that the

was on course. When he turned in that night, he left instructions that he should be awakened at 6 am, when he expected the Scillies would be showing on the radar somewhere off his starboard bow.

The chief officer, who had come on watch at 4 am, called Rugiati at 6 am and told him that the Scillies had not yet appeared. At 6.45, he called again saying that the Scillies had appeared, that they were to port rather than to starboard and he had altered course to 012 degrees.

'Who told you to make that decision?' said Rugiati. He then asked whether 018 degrees would clear the islands to the east. When the chief officer said it would, Rugiati said: 'Go back to the original course.'

ship was just 2.78 miles to the southwest of it and, to his horror, already among the rocks of the submerged reef.

When he told Rugiati, the captain ordered the helmsman to swing hard to port to miss the shallower rocks dead ahead. The helmsman turned the wheel, but the ship did not respond. Rugiati rushed over and saw that the autopilot was still engaged. He flicked the switch to manual. The helm began to respond, but that delay of one minute cost the *Torrey Canyon* her life.

Supertankers respond slowly, but she had swung around to 350 degrees when she ran into Pollard's Rock, the most northerly of the Seven Stones, at full speed. Immediately, Rugiati ordered full astern, but she was stuck fast and the rocks were tearing the bottom out of her. He sent out a distress call. The lifeboat on St Mary's (the largest of the Scilly Isles) was launched. But first on the scene was a Dutch tug called the *Utrecht*. She belonged to a salvage company called Wijsmuller of Holland, who immediately called the *Torrey Canyon's* agent in the US and suggested that they try and salvage her under a Lloyd's Open Agreement.

When she arrived, the St Mary's lifeboat ferried two salvage specialists from the *Utrecht* across to the *Torrey Canyon*. They brought with them a copy of the Lloyd's Agreement, known as a 'no cure-no pay' agreement, and asked Rugiati to sign it. If there is 'no cure', that is the wreck is not saved, the owner does not have to pay, but if the vessel is saved the owner has to cough up a large proportion of the value of the ship and cargo, as set by the arbitration committee at Lloyd's. This is often considered punitive. Rugiati took his time, saying that he was reading the small print. Meanwhile, he called his company's head office. They agreed; he signed.

The large swell made it impossible for the *Utrecht* to get alongside, but plans were laid to try

It was time for the crew to abandon ship: in a twenty-foot swell, nine crewmen jumped into the lifeboat

and pull the *Torrey Canyon* off at the next high tide that evening. Meanwhile the crew started pumping the cargo overboard to lighten her. By that evening there were five thousand tons of crude oil in the water and the slick was six miles long.

By this time, the Royal Navy had taken a hand. Lieutenant Michael Clark from the naval air station at Culdrose had been winched aboard from a helicopter. The destroyer HMS *Barrosa* was standing off and the minesweeper HMS *Clarkeston* had arrived with a thousand gallons of detergent. The situation was already looking serious. Previous oil spills in British waters had not exceeded ten thousand tons. The *Torrey Canyon* was carrying ten times that amount and was in imminent danger of breaking up. The tug *Sea Giant* was sent with another three thousand gallons of detergent to break up the oil in the water, but nothing could be done to take the stench of crude oil out of the air. Soon you could smell it as far away as Dartmoor and Torquay.

A 9 pm, there was an attempt to pull her off. It failed. At dawn she had an eight degree list to starboard. It was time for the crew to abandon ship. In a twenty-foot swell, nine crewmen jumped into the lifeboat. One fell into the sea and had to be rescued. Another nine were taken off by helicopter.

The owners flew in from America and there was a meeting in Plymouth. It was clear that the navy wanted to destroy the ship and set fire to the oil, while the owners maintained that they had a duty to try and salvage her. No one could decide whether the navy had the right to destroy a ship in international waters. Meanwhile, more ships were rushing to the stricken tanker's aid. By that evening there were eighteen ships spraying detergent into the water in the vain hope that it would break up the growing oil slick, which had reached within a few miles of Land's End.

There was a debate about the fate of the *Torrey Canyon* in the House of Commons that afternoon. The idea of transferring the oil onto another tanker was turned down as too hazardous. That night the salvors set up compressors to blow air into the *Torrey Canyon's* tanks and give her some buoyancy. But it forced more oil, along with the seawater out through the hole in her hull.

The following dawn Captain Stal and fourteen men from Wijsmuller began readying the *Torrey Canyon* for another attempt to float her off with the high tide that afternoon. This was dangerous work as the lighter fraction of the crude was evaporating, filling the ship with vapour. At noon a spark in the engine room set off a terrific explosion. Five men were injured by flying metal. Two more were blown into the sea. One was plucked from the sea by the tug standing alongside, but they could not reach Captain Stal who was unconscious. Sixty-six-year-old Captain Percy, an adviser with the oil company, leapt into the sea and, with the help of two Dutch salvage workers, manhandled Captain Stal up the ladder onto the deck of the *Torrey Canyon*. A doctor flown in from Culdrose said Stal must immediately be taken to hospital. He was transferred to a tug, but died before reaching Penzance.

That afternoon, Rugiati asked to be taken off too and left the ship in the hands of the salvage company, who still believed the ship could be saved. Although admiralty salvage experts thought the *Torrey Canyon* was doomed, the British government sent a helicopter to lift a heavy compressor sent by Wijsmuller on board. There were spring tides on the 26th, 27th and 28th of March and the Wijsmuller salvors were confident they could lift her off then. The problem was where to take her? Fearful of pollution, the government said that they would refuse her entry to any British port.

On Friday the 25th oil began lapping ashore on the beaches of Cornwall. The army was standing by. The navy was given permission to spray within three hundred yards of the shore. The local authorities were to take over from there using private boats.

On Saturday the 26th, the compressors were turned full on as the spring tide gave the salvors an extra six feet of water. At 5.40 pm, just before high tide, three tugs pulled at the great hulk, but failed to shift her. The pinnacle of Pollard's Rock had pierced the hull just forward of the bridge and no amount of pulling would get her off. Unwilling to admit defeat, Wijsmuller tried again the following day, using four tugs. But it was blowing a gale and it was late afternoon before the towlines could be attached. The cables from the two largest tugs parted and this final attempt was doomed to failure.

That afternoon, Prime Minister Harold Wilson arrived in Plymouth for a meeting. He had a holiday home on the Isles of Scilly. There was a lot of discussion about what to do if they got the *Torrey Canyon* off, which, by now, was impossible. That evening a helicopter pilot from the destroyer HMS *Delight* reported that the *Torrey Canyon's* stern was deeper in the water. When he went in closer, he noticed that the bows were sinking too. The *Torrey Canyon* was humped in the middle. In the strong winds and high seas, she had broken her back and the rest of the oil was pouring out.

On Tuesday the 28th, the owners conceded that she was lost. Wijsmuller took off its equipment and withdrew its tugs. Finally she broke into three pieces and oil poured from the tanks that had previously been intact. Rescuing any of the oil was now out of the question. The only thing to do was to set it alight. But no one had any idea whether crude oil would burn if it was floating on a rough sea. An experiment was conducted on a pond in Sussex. A thousand gallons of crude oil was poured onto it, making a slick an inch thick. Wind and waves were simulated by the exhaust of a jet engine. Then the oil was ignited. It burnt completely.

That afternoon, the last of the salvage team were taken off. The Fleet Air Arm sent Buccaneers from Lossiemouth to drop forty-one 1,000-pound bombs on the wreck – an estimated thirty actually hit the ship. Royal Air Force Hunter jets then dropped cans of aviation fuel – 5,400 gallons of it – to make sure the oil caught fire. Soon the wreck was ablaze, but little of the slick caught fire.

On the pond in Sussex, a special device called an oxygen tile had been used to ignite the floating oil. This was a flat plastic-coated sheet filled with sodium chlorate which was ignited by running an electric current through it. The navy decided to tow one of these behind a helicopter over the slick. They would start from the landward end to try and get the oil to burn back towards the wreck.

But the slick would not light. It seems, with the churning action of the sea, the flammable fraction of the crude had evaporated.

Next day, the RAF bombed the wreck again. This time, as well as dropping 62,000 gallons of aviation fuel, the Hunters also fired rockets. Napalm was tried too. But they could not get the wreck to ignite. On Thursday the 30th, Royal Navy Vixens joined the Buccaneers and Hunters dropping a hundred thousand pounds of explosive on the tangled wreck of the *Torrey Canyon* – but still no fire. They came to the conclusion that all the oil in the wreck had been burnt off. This was later confirmed by Royal Navy divers who made a

The Amoco Cadiz *breaks her back and spills her lethal cargo onto the Men Goulven Rocks, off the Brittany coast*

hazardous inspection of the wreck. They were also looking for unexploded bombs as pilots claimed some had failed to detonate. The divers found none and concluded that these must have missed.

Some fifty thousand tons of oil had already escaped. One ton of crude is 7.3 barrels, or 306.6 gallons. The slick covered 270 square miles. A hundred miles of the English coastline was contaminated. There were fears that beaches all the way up to Dover would be covered in oil. Some even reached the Hook of Holland. Two thousand British troops and a similar number of civilian volunteers set to work cleaning the beaches. Booms were used to keep the oil out of river estuaries. The US air force sent eighty-six of its men and thirty-four vehicles to help in the hazardous business of spraying the rocks around the Cornish coast. It is estimated that 25,000 birds perished in Cornwall alone.

In France over three thousand troops were sent to shovel up the 'mousse' caused by oil when mixed with seawater. By 14 April a hundred miles of holiday beaches and the Breton oyster beds were polluted. The Cornish beaches were cleared by the beginning of June; those in the Channel Isles in July, and the French beaches in August. The oyster beds eventually recovered.

A Liberian board of enquiry, which met in Genoa and London, blamed the wreck on Captain Rugiati's decision to take the supertanker through the channel between the Scillies and the Seven Stones, which is only twelve miles wide – while the channel to the west, between the Scillies and Land's End, is twenty-one miles wide. The wreck cost the underwriters £10 million, but the real cost was to the environment. And worse was to come

The next supertanker to come to grief was the Spanish-built *Amoco Cadiz*, a very large crude oil carrier built to carry between the Persian Gulf and Europe. Like the *Torrey Canyon*, she carried a

Liberian flag and an Italian crew. In early February 1978, she loaded 121,157 tons of crude oil at Ras Tanara, Saudi Arabia, and another 98,640 tons at Kharg Island, Iran. She left the Gulf on 7 February, heading for Rotterdam, via Lyme Bay, where tankers made a customary stop to lighten their load so that they could pass through the shallow waters of the eastern end of the Channel.

Slowed by three days of heavy weather in the Bay of Biscay, she was due into Lyme Bay on 16 March. As she rounded Ushant at dawn, the visibility was low. A south-westerly gale was blowing. The winds were force seven, gusting to ten, and waves were breaking over the bow. Some oil barrels were swept off the deck and Captain Pasquale Bandari, a graduate of the naval college at Pisa and former liner captain, made a number of tricky manoeuvres in the high sea to collect them. He then had to make another quick turn to avoid a small tanker that was heading south in the northbound sea lane. All the time, the wind and waves were pushing him towards the coast.

By 9.16 am, the *Amoco Cadiz* was about eight miles north of Ushant and fifteen miles from the French coast when her steering gear failed with the rudder jammed hard to port. Almost immediately Captain Bandari hoisted the international signal for 'Not Under Command' – two black balls. The wind then veered to the northwest, blowing the tanker directly onto the shore. He cut the engines and the ship slowed, but she continued on her way for another two-and-a-half miles before coming to a halt at 10.05. Once she had stopped, she slewed round in a south-easterly direction, towards the shore, rolling heavily.

His chief engineer inspected the damage. The hydraulic system had failed and he tried to fix it. When he found he could not, he tried to fix the rudder amidships with a chain, so they could at least travel directly forward or aft. But the chain

> Like the *Torrey Canyon*, the *Amoco Cadiz* carried a Liberian flag and an Italian crew

broke. The rudder now flapped with the waves and nothing could be done. At 11 am, Bandari called the coastguard at Brest and requested assistance. The German salvage tug *Pacific*, under command of Captain Hartmut Weinert, was nearby in the Chenal du Four, between Ushant and the coast. She was on her way to help another tug towing an oil rig in the Channel. Responding to the call for assistance, she arrived at 12.20. Weinert wanted to salvage the *Amoco Cadiz* under a Lloyd's Agreement, but Bandari insisted that he only wanted a tow. The first cable was secured using a Konsberg gun at 1.36 pm. But they made little way. The officers on board the *Amoco Cadiz* thought that the *Pacific* was not pulling hard enough – in fact, she was pulling at 80 per cent of her maximum power. Weinert had the throttle back as he did not want to risk snapping the towline. They were now less than six miles from Ushant. At 2.35, the *Pacific* stopped altogether and again Weinert asked whether he could salvage the *Amoco Cadiz* under a Lloyd's Agreement. When he was told to contact Amoco's headquarters in Chicago, Weinert threatened to release the towline. The situation was not helped by the fact that Bandari could not speak German and Weinert very little Italian. They communicated in English via Leslie Maynard, a Maritime Safety Services expert who had joined the *Amoco Cadiz* by helicopter at Las Palmas to give the crew instruction in safety procedures and fire-fighting.

Weinert continued to insist on a salvage agreement and Bandari tried to contact Amoco in Chicago. When he finally got through Amoco agreed to a salvage, but Weinert would not take Bandari's word for this. He insisted that Bandari make an open broadcast via the Brest coastguard radio station saying that he agreed to a 'Lloyds Open Salvage Agreement, no cure, no pay'. An hour-and-a-half had been wasted and all the time the *Amoco Cadiz* was getting closer to the coast.

Weinert now throttled up his engines, but at 5.19 pm the towline parted. There was a disagree-ment about the cause of the break. As *Amoco Cadiz* drifted towards the shore, Bandari dropped the port anchor, but it did not hold. A second, more powerful tug, the *Pacific's* sister ship *Simson*, was on its way, so the *Pacific* only had to hold the *Amoco Cadiz* off the coast for a few hours. Weinert wanted to try attaching a line to the stern, but Bandari was against this. He wanted the *Pacific* to pull the *Amoco Cadiz's* bow around to point her away from the French coast so she could use her engines to keep her off the shore. If she was being towed from aft he would have to cut his engines or risk fouling the cable and be completely dependent on the power of the *Pacific*. Then a capstan broke, filling the forecastle with steam. A second tow was secured at 8.55 pm, but the sheer mass of *Amoco Cadiz* in the teeth of a force ten made it impossi-ble for *Pacific* to do more than slow the ship's coastward drift.

At 9.04, the *Amoco Cadiz* touched bottom for the first time, and her hull and storage tanks were ripped open filling the cabins with an explosive mixture of oil-vapour and air. Everything had to be shut down for fear of a spark. Half an hour later she stuck fast on Men Goulven Rocks, twelve miles north of the port of Portsall and three miles off the coast of Brittany. The engine room flooded and the engines exploded sending flames shooting from her funnel. The port lifeboat was readied.

At 10 pm, the tow cable parted and a huge wave broke her back in two places. Her crew was rescued by helicopter at midnight. Bandari and Maynard stayed behind in case the *Simson* showed up. With the cabins filling with oil vapour, they went outside on deck where they saw sparks. On closer inspection they saw that where the ship was snagged on rocks, she was breaking in two. They searched around for a life raft, but they had been washed overboard. They found life jackets though – and some flares. Firing these they saw that the *Simson* had arrived. But it was too late. Nothing could be done and at 5.10 am another helicopter arrived to take them off.

At 10 am on 17 March, the vessel broke in two, spilling the entire cargo of 223,000 tons of crude oil into the sea. This was four times the amount lost by the *Torrey Canyon*. After the *Torrey Canyon*, the French had worked out a plan to deal with an oil spill called the Polmar plan, but no one had envisaged a spill of this magnitude. A slick eight miles wide and eight miles long polluted some 200 miles of Brittany coastline. Fisheries, oyster and seaweed beds were destroyed. Seventy-six Breton beaches were covered with oil and ten thousand French soldiers were sent to clean them. Nearly 20,000 dead birds were collected and the sand was contaminated to a depth of 20 inches.

The storm continued to pound the ship. On 28 March she broke into three pieces and the French navy destroyed the wreck with depth charges.

Ten years later a US federal court ordered Amoco Oil Corporation to pay $85 million – $45 million for the costs of the spill and $40 million in interest. The disaster also resulted in a change to the 'no cure-no pay' clause of the Lloyd's Agreement. Salvage vessels now get compensation to cover their expenses if the environment is at risk.

Just after midnight on 24 March 1989, the *Exxon Valdez* tanker hit Bligh Reef in the Prince William Sound, Alaska, dumping eleven million gallons of crude oil into its pristine waters. This was the worst oil spill in US history, though it ranked only tenth on a worldwide scale and was only one-seventh of the size of the *Amoco Cadiz* spill.

At almost a thousand feet long and a dead weight of 211,469 tons, the *Exxon Valdez* was one of the largest vessels at sea at the time. She had been commissioned in 1986, purpose built to carry crude from the oil fields in Alaska to the refineries of the Pacific coast. This should not have been necessary: when the Alaska oilfields were discovered in 1968, the consortium formed to exploit the

At 9.04, the *Amoco Cadiz* touched bottom for the first time, and her hull and storage tanks were ripped open

find proposed building a pipeline from Alaska to the oil refineries of the Midwest. The problem was that it would pass through Canadian territory and the Canadians could not see what benefit there would be for them. Instead the consortium built a pipeline to the upper reaches of Prince William Sound with a terminal at Valdez, from where the oil would be carried down the coast by tanker.

In 1987, thirty-year-old Joseph Hazelwood had been appointed skipper of the *Exxon Valdez*. He had had his master's ticket for eight years and had been in and out of Port Valdez many times. Just ten years out of New York State Maritime College he had taken command of the *Exxon Philadelphia* and, by the time of the accident, was still the youngest captain in the Exxon fleet. Under him, there was a crew of twenty-one, half the number on the *Amoco Cadiz*.

With loading completed, promptly at 11 pm on the night of 23 March 1989, the *Exxon Valdez* cast off from the terminal and manoeuvred clear of the berth under the con of the pilot Ed Murphy. She proceeded down the Valdez Narrows and along the Valdez Arm, the channel that connects the port to Prince William Sound.

The pilot was dropped off at 11.25 pm at Rocky Point. The third mate, thirty-eight-year-old Gregory Cousins was officer of the watch and he accompanied Murphy out onto the deck and stowed the pilot ladder once he had left the ship. In the ten minutes Cousins was off the bridge, Hazelwood increased to sea speed. But the outbound lane of the channel was filled with ice – so-called 'bergy bits' that can be the size of a house, and smaller 'growlers', which tend to make a growling noise in the sea.

After checking with the coastguard that there was no incoming traffic, Hazelwood changed course to 200 degrees to skirt the ice to the east. A few minutes later he spotted some more ice and turned to 180 degrees. He then steadied his course and put the autopilot on.

When Cousins returned to the bridge, Hazelwood said he was going below to do some paperwork. He explained that they were approaching Busby Island to port and would pass it about a mile off. Once they got abeam and the ice was clear to starboard, Cousins should turn southwest and 'start coming back into the lanes', clearing Bligh Reef which lay two miles to the south of Busby Island. This would require skilled navigation, but Hazelwood was confident that Cousins was up to the job. He had been with Exxon for nine years and progressed swiftly up the ranks, being promoted to third mate in 1985 and impressing all those he worked with. Hazelwood had sailed with him before and specifically requested that he join the crew of the *Exxon Valdez*. Hazelwood's evaluation report on Cousins dated 12 January 1988 said that Cousins had 'excellent navigational skills'. However, it also said he had 'only average knowledge of ship handling characteristics'. He should have been relieved by Second Mate LeCain at midnight, but Cousins agreed to work late as LeCain's off-duty period had been interrupted by casting off, which required all hands.

As the *Exxon Valdez* came abeam of the light on Busby Island at 11.55 pm, Cousins was busy fixing the ship's position and the helmsman was relieved by Able Seaman Kagan. Kagan had been with Exxon for thirteen years, serving mostly as a messman. But as the company cut back on crew, he was made an ordinary seaman. When that position was phased out too, Kagan was given an able seaman's ticket because of his length of service. Although his evaluation reports noted that he was a hard worker, they also said that he lacked 'the necessary skills to do the A.B.'s job'. Kagan knew of his shortcomings. It was noted that he was 'nervous' at the prospect of being helmsman in Prince William Sound.

There seems to have been some confusion at the point where they should have made the turn. The autopilot was found to be switched on, which is unusual in confined waters where steering is done manually. Cousins was wary of the ice to starboard, and delayed making the turn for some six minutes. Travelling at twelve knots, this took them 1.2 miles south of the position where Hazelwood had wanted the turn made. The Bligh Reef was less than a mile away, dead ahead.

Cousins later claimed that he ordered ten-degree right rudder at midnight with the ice still close on his starboard side. The ship's course recorder says that there was no change in the ship's heading until a minute later. He then phoned Hazelwood and told him that he had started to make the turn, but did not volunteer that they had overshot the point at which he had been told to change course. Hazelwood assumed that his orders were being carried out, that everything was okay and that he could go back to his paperwork.

At 12.02 am, the ship had only swung ten degrees to starboard, so Cousins ordered the rudder angle to be increased to twenty degrees. The problem was, according to the manoeuvring diagram on the bridge of the *Exxon Valdez*, even if you threw the rudder hard over – thirty-five degrees – you would travel a third of a mile before the course changed as much as ten degrees. With less rudder it took even further for the course to change significantly.

Cousins ordered the helm hard over at four 12.04 am. By five 12.05, the heading had swung to 234 degrees; at six minutes past it had reached 247 degrees. However, at the beginning of the manoeuvre, Kagan said that he was told that they were going to settle on a course of between 235 degrees and 245 degrees. Now he began to turn the rudder back to slow the turn. Although the turn resumed shortly after, at 12.07, Cousins phoned Hazelwood and said: 'I think we are in serious trouble.'

Immediately afterwards there was a jolt, then another, followed by a whole series: the *Exxon*

The Exxon Valdez, *escorted through Prince William Sound, Alaska, where she would later founder*

Valdez was hard aground on the Bligh Reef.

The oil spilt out so fast that it created waves of oil three feet above the surface of the water. By the time clean-up crews arrived ten hours later, the slick covered several miles. The chemical dispersants dropped from aeroplanes depended on wave action to work and the water in the sound was too calm for them to be effective. By the third day, the oil had covered a hundred square miles. There were not enough containment booms to prevent it spreading and it was soon threatening the country's richest concentrations of wildlife. It also threatened the livelihood of the local fishing industry and native villagers, affecting about 34,000 fishermen, some 4,000 native Alaskans, and several thousand more Alaska residents.

On the afternoon and early evening of sailing, Hazelwood had had a few drinks. The pilot smelt alcohol on his breath. So did the coastguards who came on board three hours after the *Exxon Valdez* grounded. Later it was discovered that he had two convictions for drunken driving and had undergone treatment in 1985 for an alcohol problem. When this came out in the media, in the public mind it became clear that he was drunk in charge of a ship. He was charged with criminal mischief, but was acquitted.

Exxon led the clean-up effort with 11,000 workers in the summer months, spending some $2 billion dollars on the operation. A further $1 billion was spent on settling related court cases. Sea otter rehabilitation centres were established and salmon and herring fisheries were isolated and monitored. Years later, however, scientists were still attempting to determine the ecological damage caused by the spill.

6 Sunken Submarines

As well as introducing iron ships and steam-powered warfare to the seas, the US Civil War also ushered in the age of submarine warfare. It also produced the first wreck. Named the *H.L. Hunley*, she was the third of three experimental submersibles developed for the Confederacy by James McClintock and Baxter Watson.

Made from an iron steam boiler, she had tapered ends and dive planes for submerging and surfacing, internal ballast tanks connected by pumps to maintain trim and a mercury depth gauge. With a crew of nine, she was powered by hand cranks and could make up to four knots.

Prototype Confederate submarine the H.L. Hunley

Snorkels provided fresh air when the vessel was submerged.

After successful trials in Mobile Bay, the submarine was transported to Charleston where she was to be used to break the blockade. The idea was for the submarine to tow a copper mine under an enemy ship and detonate it. However, Union ships were protected by weighted nets and they rode in water too shallow for the submarine to pass under them. So the *H.L. Hunley* was fitted with a nineteen-foot metal bow spar with a barbed spike on the end and a mine filled with ninety pounds of black powder hanging from it. The spike was to be driven into the side of the wooden ship below the water line. As the submarine pulled away, a mechanism would detonate the mine, sinking the ship.

However, the submarine sank in two trials in Charleston harbour, drowning thirteen men, including the project's financial backer, the eponymous Horace L. Hunley. The first time, she went down at the dockside. All the water had not been pumped out of the ballast tanks so she was low in the water, and both the hatches had been left open. When the captain, John A. Payne, stepped onto the diving plane, the bow dipped. Water went into the hatches and she sank in forty-two feet of water.

The second time, she dived at too steep an angle and got stuck in the mud. The crew had suffocated before rescuers could free her. When she was raised

The wreck of the H.L. Hunley *is raised from her resting-place, 8 August 2000*

the second time and the hatches opened, the scene inside was 'indescribably ghastly; the unfortunate men were distorted into all kinds of horrible attitudes... the blackened faces of all presented the expression of their despair and agony.'

General Pierre Gustave Toutant Beauregard, who was organising the defence of Charleston, ordered that she should only operate on the surface after that. Even so, a new crew was assembled, under the command of Lieutenant George Dixon, and she went out on her first attack on the night of 17 February 1864. Outside Charleston harbour, she rammed the USS *Housatonic*. Spotted by a lookout, sentries opened fire on her exposed superstructure and the *Housatonic's* captain, Charles Pickering, discharged his double-barrelled shotgun into the conning tower. As the *H.L. Hunley* pulled away, the mine exploded, sinking the *Housatonic*. However, the submarine was lost too. The wreck of the *Housatonic* was surveyed nine months later and again in 1873 when the remains were to be demolished, but no sign of the *H.L. Hunley* was found. She was not located until May 1995 when she was found buried under sediment in thirty-three feet of water, just a thousand feet from the *Housatonic*, and she was eventually raised on 8 August 2000. *The H.L. Hunley* cannot be considered an unmitigated success and submarine warfare was not attempted again until World War I.

The wreck of the first mechanically powered submarine, the *Resurgam*, was found in fifty feet of water off Rhyl, North Wales, in 1995. Built in the Britannia Iron Works in Birkenhead, she was launched in 1879. The brainchild of a Victorian curate, the Reverend George Garrett, she was powered by a closed system containing superheated water that was stored at pressure, which could be released as steam to power the engine. The system gave up to four hours of steam-power without the need of a furnace, giving the vessel a top speed of three knots and a range of up to twelve miles.

Garrett also developed a system to recycle air using caustic soda, so that the crew of three could breathe, and he armed his submarine with two spring-mounted torpedoes. Eager to demonstrate his craft to the navy, in December 1879, he hired a steam yacht to tow her to Portsmouth. They were caught in a storm rounding Great Orme's Head. The crew of the submarine was taken on board the yacht, but a special safety feature incorporated in Garrett's design meant that it was impossible to close the hatch from outside. She filled with water, broke the tow cable and sank.

The search for the *Resurgam* started in 1975. The Royal Navy made a survey of the area using a magnetometer in 1981. Sonars were used in further attempts to locate her in the late 1980s and early 1990s. These were funded by George

Full-sized replica of early British submarine the Resurgam, *Birkenhead*

Garrett's great-grandson William. Then in October 1995, a fisherman's net snagged on the wreck. Divers went down and confirmed that it was the *Resurgam*, but then tried to sell details of the location. Unwilling to pay, the British Archaeological Diving Unit conducted another search and found the *Resurgam* the following year. There had been some looting of the wreck, which had been damaged, and the *Resurgam* is unlikely to live up to its name, which means 'I will rise again'.

In 1876, with backing from the Fenian Brotherhood in the US, the Irish-American inventor John Phillip Holland built a midget submarine. Then in 1881, he launched the fully realised fighting vessel, the *Fenian Ram*. Soon after, he fell out with the brotherhood, she was laid up and never saw combat. However, Holland began making a series of submarines, called Holland boats, for the US navy. Ironically the plans were then delivered to the British, who feared that they were falling behind in the race to build submarines. They commissioned *Holland I*, built under licence by Vickers at Barrow-in-Furness. Launched in October 1901, the sixty-four-foot, 122-ton submarine was powered by electric batteries and was armed with torpedoes. By 1913, she was obsolete. She was stripped of her equipment and sold for scrap. But on her way to the scrap yard, under tow, she sank off Plymouth.

In 1981, a Royal Navy minesweeper located the wreck near the Eddystone lighthouse. Navy divers raised her the following year and she was taken to Devonport where she was cleaned and conserved. She is now on display in a conservation tank at the Royal Navy's submarine museum in Gosport.

The British lost the *K-13* during a

test dive at her acceptance trials at Gareloch on 29 January 1917, due to a malfunction in the control panel. All its lights showed green, indicating that ventilation doors to the boiler room were closed. In fact, they were open and, when the submarine dived, the aft compartment filled with water and she sank. Thirty-four seamen were drowned immediately, and forty-eight others were trapped in the forward compartment. They were in sixty feet of water, meaning rescue was possible. Commander Francis Goodhart, the captain of the *K-14* who was on board as an observer, volunteered to make an escape from the conning tower and call for help. He died in the attempt, but Lieutenant-Commander Herbert who went with him reached the surface alive.

With the help of another submarine, *E-51*, a high-pressure air line was attached to the *K-13*. This was used to blow the ballast tank and the *K-13's* bows were hauled to the surface. An oxyacetylene torch was used to cut a hole in her hull and, fifty-four hours after the submarine had sunk, forty-six survivors crawled out to huge cheers.

When the hull was raised, Goodhart's body was found in the wheelhouse. It appeared that he had hit his head, knocked himself out and drowned.

The *K-13* was refitted and recommissioned as the *K-22*, but the K-class soon acquired a terrible reputation. Of the eighteen commissioned, eight suffered disasters. Sixteen were involved in major accidents and there were numerous minor incidents. The *K-22* was taken out of service and broken up on 26 December 1926.

But the sinking of the *K-13* – the first accident to befall the ill-fated K-class – served as a warning to Lieutenant-Commander Herbert. It was the fourth submarine accident he had been involved in and he never served in submarines again.

On 9 June 1931, the British submarine HMS

> **When the *K-13* dived, the aft compartment filled with water and she sank, drowning thirty-four seamen immediately**

Poseidon was rammed by the Japanese merchant steamer *Yuta* in the South China Sea, cutting a V-shaped hole in the submarine's pressure hull. She sank in two minutes in 130 feet of water. Twenty-nine men managed to scramble out of the conning tower as she went down. Eighteen men were trapped in the stern and were unable to escape.

Another eight were in the bows under the command of Petty Officer P.W. Willis, who handed out the new Davis Submarine Escape Apparatus. This primitive aqualung was supposed to allow individual crew members to breathe underwater as they made their way to the surface.

Before they could make their escape, they had to flood the compartment. This took them two-and-a-half hours. When the water was up to their necks, Willis forced the torpedo loading hatch open. Able Seamen Edmund Holt and Arthur Lovock shot to the surface. Both were picked up but Lovock died soon after. It took another three-quarters of an hour to repressurise the compartment. When Willis tried the hatch again, the remaining six escaped, though only four reached the surface alive. One was killed by hitting his head on the rim of the hatchway. The other made the mistake of holding his breath and as the water pressure diminished as he headed towards the surface his lungs burst.

The American submarine *Squalus* suffered the same mishap as Britain's *K-13*. The control panel said that all hatches were secure when, in fact, an air inlet had been left open. She partially filled with water and sank off Portsmouth, New Hampshire, on 23 May 1939 in 240 feet of water. The captain knew that rescue was possible at such a depth, so he kept his men still and quiet to conserve air. The next day a diving bell was lowered over the escape hatch. Twenty-six men had been drowned when she went down, but the remaining thirty-three escaped. The

Rescue attempts on the crippled HMS Thetis *in Liverpool Bay*

After initial trials of the *Thetis* in April 1939 failed due to the forward hydroplanes becoming jammed, preventing her from submerging, a sub-contractor of Cammell Laird had applied a substance called Bitumastic to the inside of the tubes. Unfortunately, this material had blocked the spitcock on torpedo tube number five.

Thetis sailed again on 1 June 1939 to perform sea trials in Liverpool Bay. There were 103 people on board – personnel from Cammell Laird and the sub-contractors and observers Captain H.P.K. Oram and Captain S. Jackson, as well as the regular crew. At 1.40 pm, Lieutenant-Commander Guy Bolus, commander of the *Thetis*, signalled that he was going to dive. But when the order to dive was given forty minutes later, the *Thetis* refused to sink, even though all the ballast tanks and auxiliary tanks had been flooded.

It was decided that the submarine's continued buoyancy might have been due to air in the torpedo tubes. Each tube held 1,600 pounds of water, so even if one of them was empty it could have made the difference between staying on the surface and going under.

The torpedo officer, Lieutenant Frederick Woods was sent to check the tubes. He opened the spitcocks. The first four were dry, nothing came out of five, and a trickle came out of six. Ordered to make further investigations, he checked the bow cap indicators to make sure the outer doors were closed. These were arranged vertically, but in a strange order – one, two, three, four, six and then five. The indicator for tube five was also

Squalus herself was refloated four months later.

A more tragic fate awaited those on board HMS *Thetis* the following month. Due to an error in the construction, it was possible to open the loading door to number five torpedo tube while the outer cap was open. There was also a fault with the tube's spitcock. This is a small tap at the rear of the tube that lets you test what is going on inside. If the tube is full of water and the outer door is closed, when the spitcock is opened only a little water will dribble out. But if the outer door is open, the pressure will make water spurt out of the spitcock.

partially obscured by a metal bar, and the position indicating 'shut' on indicator five was different from the rest. All the others indicated 'shut' at eleven o'clock: five indicated 'shut' at five o'clock. Woods looked down the line of indicators, saw them all aligned and assumed that all the bow caps were closed when, in fact, five's bow cap was still open. He then ordered the tubes to be opened. Leading Seaman Hambrook opened tubes one, two, three and four, but when he reached number five he found the lever to be stiff and threw his full weight against it. The door sprang open and a huge jet of water twenty-one inches in diameter came flooding in.

Realising that something was wrong, Bolus reacted by blowing the main ballast tank. This might have saved the *Thetis* had the watertight doors been closed. But the pressure of the incoming water on the door to the torpedo room made it impossible to shut. As the *Thetis* hit the bottom 150 feet down, Bolus ordered the door to the next compartment to be sealed. If water reached the batteries, deadly chlorine gas would be given off. The situation was already desperate. The forward two compartments were flooded and there were twice the normal complement of men on board.

Bolus realised that if one of the forward compartments could be drained, it would be possible for the *Thetis* to surface. He came up with a plan. Using Davis Submarine Escape Apparatus, a man would go forward and enter the second compartment through the emergency escape hatch. He would close the watertight door to the torpedo room, now that the pressure was equalised either side of it. He would then open the two main suction valves allowing the ballast pumps to expel the water. Four members of the crew tried this, but could not stand the pressure on their ears they suffered as the escape chamber filled.

> **The *Thetis* was raised on 23 October 1939 at the cost of the life of a diver, Petty Officer Henry Perdue, bringing the death toll to one hundred**

Bolus's next plan was to raise the *Thetis's* stern, bringing the aft escape hatch nearer the surface. The *Thetis* was 169 feet long and by the following morning eighteen feet of the stern was jutting above the surface.

On board the tug *Grebecock* that was accompanying the *Thetis* on her sea trials, Lieutenant L.E. Coltart had been alarmed by the speed of the submarine's dive. Then he had noted that she did not carry out any of her planned manoeuvres. At 4.15 pm he sent a message back to the flag officer at Fort Blockhouse. This did not get through until 6.15 pm, by which time the flag officer was already worried as he had not received a message from Bolus, saying that he had surfaced. A search was ordered, but nothing was found before nightfall.

At dawn the following day, the destroyer HMS *Brazen* spotted the stern of the submarine and dropped two explosive charges alongside so the occupants would know that rescue was at hand. Almost immediately two heads appeared in the water. Lieutenant Woods and Captain Oram had got out through the stern escape hatch. They were picked up. Bolus had picked Woods to go, because he had the most intimate knowledge of what had gone wrong. Oram was picked because he was the commander of Fifth Submarine Flotilla and Bolus reckoned that having the expertise of a senior submarine officer on the surface might help the rescuers. Oram brought with him detailed notes from the *Thetis's* engineering officer explaining how to salvage the submarine. He also brought the message for those on the surface to keep a constant eye out for those escaping from the aft chamber.

At 10 am, Cammell Laird fitter Frank Shaw and Leading Stoker Walter Arnold bobbed to the surface. They reported that conditions inside the

Thetis were dire. The air was almost exhausted. But worse was to come. After Shaw and Arnold left, the escape chamber was being drained, ready for another escape. Exhausted and starved of oxygen, the rating working the chamber failed to release the gearing on the upper hatch, making it impossible to open it from the inside. Four men who tried to use the chamber were dragged out dead or dying.

Two more men tried to use the escape chamber. They also failed to open the outer hatch. But when they clambered back into the motor room, they failed to close the flooding valve. For the second time in twenty-four hours the *Thetis* was open to the sea. The water cascading in increased the carbon dioxide concentration, asphyxiating the ninety-nine men left on board before they drowned.

That morning, the flotilla of ships that surrounded the stern of the *Thetis* did nothing but look on. When it was clear that no more men were coming out of the aft escape chamber, Wreckmaster Brock climbed onto the stern. His plan was to open a manhole into Z tank, then climb through the tank into the steering machinery compartment. Just as he started to free the covering plate, the *Thetis* began to twist in the tide and he was washed off. Next, the salvage ship *Vigilant* came alongside with equipment to cut a hole in the submarine's hull. But the force of the tide proved too strong. At 3.10 pm, the cables parted and the *Thetis* disappeared from sight. Ninety-nine men had perished and a horrified public saw footage of her loss on the newsreels.

The *Thetis* was raised on 23 October 1939 at the cost of the life of a diver, Petty Officer Henry Perdue, bringing the death toll to one hundred. In peacetime, she would probably have been broken up. But World War II had started and Britain needed every submarine she could get. Her hull alone was worth £300,000 to the hard-pressed Treasury. She was recommissioned under the name HMS *Thunderbolt*. On 14 March 1943,

Thunderbolt was depth-charged by the Italian destroyer *Cicogna*. As she went down, her stern once again stood at ninety degrees out of the water. A second run of depth charges blew her out of the water and she sank. Two more depth charges brought oil and debris to the surface.

The wreck lay undisturbed at the bottom of the Mediterranean until she was discovered on 9 November 1995. Lying upright on the bottom wreathed in fishing nets and wires, her hydroplanes were set at hard to dive and there was a large hole on the port side just forward of the conning tower. To confirm her identification, a diver took a photograph of a bronze plate on her four-in gun. The inscription read: '*Thetis* No. 1027' – 1027 was the yard number given to the *Thetis* by Cammell Laird.

Nuclear submarines

After World War II the age of the nuclear submarine dawned. One of the first was the USS *Thresher*. Commissioned in 1961, she was 278.5 feet long and her single nuclear reactor and two steam turbines driving one screw gave her a top speed of thirty knots underwater and twenty knots on the surface. In 1962, she went to Portsmouth Naval Shipyard, New Hampshire for a refit. There she got a new captain, Lieutenant-Commander John Harvey, previously executive officer of the *Sea Dragon*. The *Thresher* was his first command.

The refit complete, Harvey took the *Thresher* and her crew of 129 men out on sea trials on 9 April 1963. She rendezvoused with the support vessel *Skylark* two hundred miles east of Cape Cod. At 7.47 on the morning of 10 April, the *Thresher* was at periscope depth when Harvey told the *Skylark* via the underwater telephone that she was going down to test depth. (The test depth is the maximum depth that a submarine can work and fight, and is not exceeded except in an emergency. Beyond this the hull is compressed and things bolted to the bulkheads begin to come away. The hull then begins to distort, springs leaks and is eventually crushed like an orange.) Just how deep the test depth was, was top secret. It was never divulged even in sea trials in case enemy vessels were listening in. There were no scramblers on underwater phones. However, the *Thresher* had regularly been to test depth before the refit so, for the crew, this was routine.

At 7.52 am the *Thresher* told the *Skylark* that she was at four hundred feet and was checking for leaks. Seventeen minutes later she reported that she was at half the test depth. At 8.35 am, she said she was still three hundred feet above the test depth and at 8.53 am she said she was 'proceeding to test depth'. There were further routine communications at 9.02 am and 9.12 am. A minute later Lieutenant Watson, who was manning the telephone on the *Skylark*, heard the *Thresher* say: 'Have positive up angle' – which

Early US nuclear submarine USS Thresher *undergoing sea trials in 1963*

means the submarine was out of trim. Then he heard: 'Am attempting to blow'. This means they were going to blow compressed air into the ballast tanks which would bring the submarine to the surface.

A garbled message was received at 9.17 am. Then Lieutenant Watson said he heard 'the sound of a ship breaking up'. These sounds would have been all too grimly familiar to Watson. He had served as a sonar operator in the navy during World War II and had frequently heard the sounds of submarines breaking up.

Watson continued trying to communicate with the sub but received no reply. The *Skylark* then started a search and dropped grenades to indicate

that, although communication had been lost, she was still there.

The *Skylark* also sent a signal to the commander of the Second Submarine Flotilla, who received it when he got back from lunch. Although he was not unduly worried he passed the message on to Admiral Elton W. Grenfell, commander of all the submarines in the Atlantic. Grenfell ordered the nuclear submarine *Seawolf* to the scene, along with the conventional submarine *Sea Owl*, the frigate *Norfolk* and a variety of other rescue ships. The matter was also reported upwards to the Chief of Naval Operations, the Secretary of the Navy and to President John F. Kennedy, himself an ex-navy man.

As the Thresher's last known position was a hundred miles off Nova Scotia, the Canadian navy was also asked for assistance. In turn, they asked a British submarine that was visiting Halifax to help. Most members of her crew were on shore leave, so messages asking them to return to ship were flashed on the screen in Halifax's cinemas, alerting the press.

That evening, as the weather began to close in, the rescue ship *Recovery* spotted a calm patch in the increasingly choppy seas. It was oil. Although the *Thresher* did not carry fuel oil, there would have been lubricating oil on board. Bits of cork and heavy yellow plastic of the type used on submarines were also recovered.

At 8 pm, the Department of Defense made a formal announcement that the *Thresher* had been lost and the crew's next of kin were contacted. At 9.30 pm, Chief of Naval Operations Admiral George W. Anderson went on television saying that the *Thresher* had gone down in over eight thousand feet of water and that 'rescue would be absolutely out of the question'.

But the search for the wreck of the *Thresher* continued. It was not only the Americans who were looking for her: on several occasions, Soviet ships strayed into the area and had to be warned off. When all conventional ways of finding the sunken submarine had been exhausted, the US navy flew in the bathyscaphe *Trieste* which was designed for deep oceanographic work. After two-and-a-half months of searching the sea floor she found a patch of scattered debris, but no human remains. One piece of the wreckage brought to the surface was inscribed '593 boat'. The *Thresher* had been designated SSN-593. It was part of the *Thresher*.

The *Thresher's* former captain, Commander Axene told a court of enquiry that her first test dive – in the same area as she had been lost – had to be halted when a number of instruments failed. He also said that, in his opinion, the loss of the *Thresher* must have been 'associated with some flooding problem'.

Lieutenant-Commander McCoole, an officer from the *Thresher* who had been left ashore because his wife was ill, said that there were problems with the air system. Twenty per cent of the hydraulic valves were installed back to front. There were also problems with her periscope, and her diving planes and rudder were found to be faulty and parts had had to be replaced before her last dive. A test in the dockyard had also failed when the submarine's ventilation system broke down.

The court of enquiry concluded:

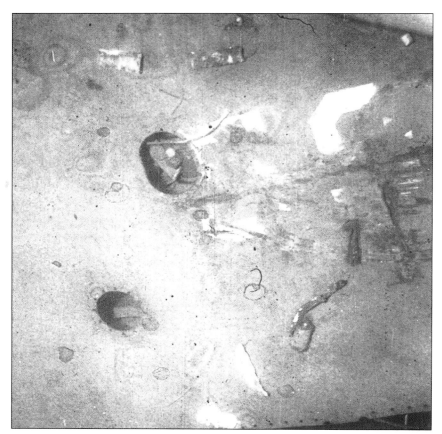

The wreck of the Thresher. *Part of her number can be seen to the right*

The US Navy bathyscape Trieste, *designed for work in the ocean depths, eventually located the wreck of the* Thresher

'The navy believes it most likely that a piping failure had occurred in one of the *Thresher's* saltwater systems, probably in the engine room. The enormous pressure of sea water surrounding the submarine subjected her interior to a violent spray of water and progressive flooding. In all probability water affected electrical circuits and caused loss of power. *Thresher* slowed and began to sink. Within minutes she had exceeded her collapse depth and was totally flooded. She came to rest on the ocean floor 8,400 feet beneath the surface.'

The following month, the US navy lost another nuclear submarine, the USS *Scorpion*. She was last heard from travelling underwater off the Azores on 21 May. When she did not arrive in Norfolk, Virginia, as expected on 27 May a large-scale search was made. The records were checked at the navy's secret underwater listening station and a recording was found of what appeared to be an underwater implosion shortly after the *Scorpion's* last transmission four hundred miles southwest of San Miguel in the Azores, near the *Scorpion's* last known position. The sound was thought to be that of a ship being crushed by water pressure at two thousand feet. At that time, it was thought that she had run into a seamount, or underwater volcano.

In November 1968, a ship fitted with remote video cameras located the wreck and photographed it. But this provided no conclusive evidence as to why it had sunk. At that time, the leading theory was that she had some piping problem in her deballasting system. But in 1993, the navy issued a report saying that they believed one of the *Scorpion's* torpedoes had somehow become armed. In an effort to save the submarine it was fired out of the torpedo tube, but had turned and homed in on the mother ship, sinking her.

The Soviet Union also lost a submarine that year, the *K129*, a Golf class nuclear missile carrier with seventy crew on board. She was being tracked by the American underwater listening station on Hawaii when she suddenly disappeared. Soon the Pacific was full of Soviet vessels looking for her. This alerted the Americans to the fact that she was important. As the Soviets searched the huge ocean, it became clear that they did not know where she was. But the Americans did: 1,700 miles northwest of Hawaii and three miles down. They figured that if she had flooded before she went down, she would not have been crushed by the water pressure, in which case it might be possible to salvage her safe, which would be full of valuable codes, and the latest Soviet missiles from her silos.

This had to be done discreetly, so an old submarine, the USS *Halibut*, was fitted with an array of modern electronics and sent to look for her. She found the *K129* lying on the seabed 'as if parked there'. There was a huge hole behind the conning tower. Experts concluded that hydrogen, built up when charging the batteries, had exploded. The rest of the submarine looked intact and there was still a missile in one of her silos. More gruesomely,

there was a skeleton beside the submarine, whose leg had been broken in the three-mile fall to the seabed. Another body, that of a young sailor, was being eaten by worms. He was wearing waterproofs, indicating that the submarine was on the surface when she went down.

Plans were made to send down a remote-controlled mini-sub and raise the safe and the warhead. Then the CIA came up with an audacious plan to raise the entire submarine. In 1974, they hired the *Glomar Explorer*, a state-of-the-art deep-sea exploration vessel designed to raise valuable minerals from the sea floor, owned by the increasingly eccentric Howard Hughes. But security had been breached. Just before the operation was to go ahead, an office building owned by Hughes was broken into by four masked men who took money and classified documents. A note outlining the CIA's plan was pushed through the letter box of the Soviet Embassy in Washington. But as the Soviets did not have the technology to work at depths of 16,000 feet, they dismissed it as a hoax and went on believing that the *K129* was safe under three miles of water.

Even though the mission had been compromised, the CIA decided to go ahead anyway. The *Glomar Explorer* sailed out over the wreck and dropped a grab. This seized hold of the submarine and began to raise it. But metal gets extremely brittle at those depths. The middle section of the submarine came away and a nuclear missile fell back, harmlessly, to the sea floor. The bulk of the vessel was raised, however, and six bodies that were found in the wreckage were later buried with all due ceremony.

The New York Times broke the story in 1975, but the Soviets approached President Ford to discuss the situation. The salvage operation was an embarrassment to both sides and they agreed to hush it up. A video tape of the burial of the Soviet sailors from the *K129* was given to Russian president Boris Yeltsin after the end of the Cold War and the collapse of the Soviet Union.

The Kursk *undergoes sea trials in the Barents Sea. None of her 118 crewmen survived the sinking on 12 August 2000*

Grey Lady Down

The worst submarine loss in recent memory was the sinking of the Russian nuclear submarine *Kursk* in the Barents Sea on 12 August 2000. She went down with 118 crewmen on board some hundred miles northwest of Murmansk. The submarine was located at about 5 am the following day. Rescue vessels arrived in the area soon after. Two attempts were made to save the trapped submariners, but the rescue craft were unable to dock with the submarine.

The *Kursk* crewmen were still alive at 14 August and signalling that there was water inside – though it was thought that most of the crew had been killed immediately by an explosion or the original inrush of water. But it was not until the 16th that the Russians requested British and American help to rescue any survivors. By then, all the crewmen were dead.

Further attempts to dock with the submarine failed. But on 21 August, Norwegian divers managed to open the external hatch of the submarine, but found no sign of life.

In October the following year, the *Kursk* was lifted from the sea floor. By the end of March 2002, the bodies of 115 of the crewmen had been found and identified. A government investigation concluded that a training torpedo had gone off, detonating other torpedoes stockpiled in the forward compartment of the submarine. Men towards the aft had survived for some time in air pockets but the Russian authorities' reluctance to call for help sealed their fate.

On Friday 3 November 2000, the first of the funerals for victims of the *Kursk* disaster was held, when the burial of Lieutenant-Captain Dmitri Kolesnikov took place. A passage from the note he wrote while he waited to die in the hours after the accident was displayed in a frame by the closed coffin. The family had still not been given either the original or a photocopy of the note, but Kolesnikov's father had been shown it and had made an unauthorized transcription. It read: '15.45. It's dark to write here, I'm trying to write blindly. It seems we have no chance – no more than 10 to 20 per cent. I hope at least that some-one will read this. Here is a list of the crew who are in the ninth compartment and will try to get out... Hello to everyone, there is no need to despair.'

Speaking at the funeral Northern Fleet Commander Vyacheslav Popov, praised Kolesnikov for his bravery, saying: 'His fate will become an example of serving the fatherland for everyone.'

A post-mortem established that Kolesnikov had died from carbon monoxide poisoning.

Workers pump water out of the raised Kursk *submarine, Roslyakovo Shipyard, Russia, 29 October 2001*

7 Perils of the Sea

The sea is a dangerous place, even now. But in the days of sail before scientific weather forecasting had been invented, shipping was in constant danger of unexpected storms. In the Caribbean, for example, there were no bad weather warnings and the New Spain Fleet lost treasure ships in hurricanes in 1589, 1590, 1600, 1610, 1615, 1631, 1641, 1715 and 1725, littering the sea floor with gold.

Of all the storms that have hit the Caribbean, the Great Hurricane of 1780 is believed to be the most deadly. It is estimated that some 22,000 people died as it swept across Martinique, St. Lucia, St. Vincent, St. Kitts, Grenada and Barbados. At sea the Royal Navy lost the seventy-four-gun *Thunderer*, the sixty-four-gun *Stirling Castle*, the forty-two-gun *La Blanche*, the twenty-eight-gun *Laurel*, the twenty-eight-gun *Andromeda*, the twenty-four-gun *Deal Castle*, the twenty-gun *Scarborough*, the sixteen-gun *Beaver's Prize*, the fourteen-gun *Barbados*, the ten-gun *Victor*, and the forty-four-gun *Phoenix*, commanded by Sir Hyde Parker who would be Nelson's superior at the Battle of Copenhagen. It was Parker's signal to disengage from the enemy that Nelson so famously ignored by raising a telescope to his blind eye and saying: 'I see no ships.' Also on board the *Phoenix* at the time she was lost was Lieutenant Archer, who wrote to his mother about the shipwreck.

HMS *Phoenix:* A Survivor's Account

According to Archer's account, the *Phoenix* left Port Royal, Jamaica, bound for Pensacola, Florida, accompanied by two store ships, on 2 August 1780. From there they were going to cruise off Havana and patrol in the Gulf of Mexico for six weeks. It was an uneventful trip. The crew did little but catch fish and gamble, scarcely even catching sight of any other vessel. In search of action, they set sail back to Cape San Antonio at the western end of Cuba, where they saw a fleet of Spanish merchant ships. But when they went in to attack them, they found the merchant ships were guarded by three Spanish ships of the line. The *Phoenix* made a run for it and she was too fast for the Spanish ships to catch.

They stopped another ship, but it turned out to be the *Polly* on its way to New York. So the *Phoenix* turned back towards Port Royal empty-handed. She was rounding Cape San Antonio when a tremendous wind hit. Everyone got sea sick – 'all of us as green as you please' – then a lookout spotted breakers: *Phoenix* was being blown onto a lee shore, a very dangerous situation for ships wholly dependent on the wind for their motion. The *Phoenix* managed to claw her way off the shore, but the squalls she had sailed through were an ominous foretaste of things to come.

On 30 September the *Phoenix* set sail from Montego Bay on Jamaica to Port Royal in Kingston Bay, around the eastern end of the island. On the evening of 2 October, they were hit by a heavy wind from the east and the *Phoenix* close reefed the topsails. Parker sent for Archer and asked him what the weather was like.

Archer said: 'It blows a little, and has a very ugly look; if in any other quarter but this, I would say we were going to have a gale of a wind.'

Parker agreed, but thought that it was best to keep the topsails lashed until the wind dropped.

Archer was relieved at twelve. It was a rough night and when he came on deck the following morning there were heavy squalls. Parker again asked Archer what he made of the weather.

'The clouds are beginning to break,' he said, ever optimistic. 'It will clear up at noon, or else blow very hard afterwards.'

'I wish it would clear up,' said Parker, 'but I doubt it very much. I was once in a hurricane in the East Indies, and the beginnings of it have much the same appearance as this. So take in the topsails, we have plenty of sea room.'

Parker was right. The weather did not clear up at noon. Archer wrote to his mother:

At twelve, the gale still increasing, wore ship, to keep as near mid-channel, between Jamaica and Cuba, as possible; at one the gale increasing still; at two harder! Reefed the courses, and furled them; brought to under a foul mizzen staysail, head to the northward. In the evening no sign of the weather taking off, but every appearance of the storm increasing, prepared for a proper gale of wind; secured all the sails with spare gaskets; good rolling tackles upon the yards; squared the booms; saw the boats made fast; new lashed the guns; double breeched the lower decks; saw that the carpenters had the tarpaulins and battens all ready for the hatchways; got the top-gallant-mast down upon the deck; jib-boom and sprit-sail-yard fore and aft; in fact, did everything we could think of to make a snug ship.

If the situation was not worrying enough, nature provided its own omen of what was about to befall them.

The poor devils of birds now began to find the uproar in the elements, for numbers, both of sea and land kinds, came on board of us. I took notice of some, which happening to be to leeward, turned to windward, like a ship, tack and tack; for they could not fly against it. When they came over to the ship they dashed themselves down upon the deck, without attempting to stir till picked up, and when let to again, they would not leave the ship, but endeavoured to hide themselves from the wind.

They now faced nightfall in this appalling weather, and the situation immediately began to worsen:

At eight o'clock a hurricane; the sea roaring, but the wind still steady to a point; did not ship a spoonful of water. However, got the hatchways all secured, expecting what would be the consequence should the wind shift; placed the carpenters by the mainmast, with broad axes, knowing from experience that, at the moment you may want to cut it away to save the ship, an axe may not be found. Went to supper; bread, cheese and porter. The purser frightened to bits about his bread bags; the two marine officers as white as sheets, not understanding the ship's working so much, and the noise of the lower deck guns; which, by this time, made a pretty screeching to the people not used to it; it seemed as if the whole ship's side was going at each roll. Wooden, our carpenter, was all this time smoking his pipe and laughing at the doctor; the second lieutenant upon deck; and the third in his hammock...
At ten o'clock I thought to get a little sleep; came to look into my cot; it was full of water; for every seam, by the straining of the ship, had begun to leak. Stretched myself, therefore, upon deck, between two chests, and left orders to be called should the least thing happen.
At twelve a midshipman came to me:
"Mr Archer, we are just going to wear ship, sir!"

"O, very well, I'll be up directly; what sort of weather have you got?"
"It blows a hurricane."
Went upon deck, found Sir Hyde there.
"It blows damn'd hard, Archer."
"It does indeed, sir."

After a consultation with his captain, Archer ordered about two hundred sailors into the fore rigging and, after a hard struggle, managed to wear ship. But he soon found she did not sail so well on this tack as on the other. The sea began to run across her and she had not risen from one wave, before another dashed across her.

Began to think we should lose our masts, as the ship lay very much along, by the pressure of the wind constantly upon the yards and masts alone: for the poor mizzen staysail had gone in shreds long before, and the sails began to fly from the yards through the gaskets into coach whips. My God! To think that the wind could have such force...
Sir Hyde now sent me to see what was the matter between decks as there was a good deal of noise. As soon as I was below, one of the marine officers calls out: "Good God! Mr Archer, we are sinking, the water is up to the bottom of my cot."
"Pooh, pooh! As long as it is not over your mouth, you are well off; what the devil do you make this noise for?"
I found some water between decks, but nothing to be alarmed at: scuttled [bailed out] the deck, and it ran into the well; found she made a good deal of water through the sides and decks; turned the watch below to the pumps, though only two feet of water in the well; but expected to be kept constantly at work now, as the ship laboured so much, with scarcely a part of her above water but the quarter-deck, and that but seldom.
While I was standing at the pumps, cheering the people, the carpenter's mate came running to me with a face as long as my arm: "O, Sir! The ship has sprung a leak in the gunner's room."

Archer then had a private word with the carpenter, told him to go and inspect the leak and report back to him privately, not to alarm anyone. Shortly the carpenter returned and said: 'Sir, there is nothing there, it is only the water washing up between the timbers that this booby has taken for a leak.'

Archer then ordered the carpenter to go up on deck and see if he could stop the water washing into the cabins.

"Sir, I have had four people constantly keeping the hatchways secure," said the carpenter, "but there is such a weight of water upon the deck that nobody can stand it when the ship rolls."

The gunner then showed Archer that the bottom layer of gunpowder in the magazine was soaked. But he insisted that this was not his fault; he had stowed the powder properly, and he begged Archer to speak to Parker and let him know this.

I could not forbear smiling to see how easy he took the danger of the ship, and said to him, let us shake off this gale of wind first, and talk of the damaged powder afterwards...
At four, we had gained upon the ship a little, and I went upon deck, it being my watch. The second lieutenant relieved me at the pumps. Who can attempt to describe the appearance of things upon deck? If I was to write forever, I could not give you an idea of it – a total darkness all above; the sea on fire, running as it were in Alps, or Peaks of Tenerife (mountains are too common an idea); the wind roaring louder than thunder (absolutely no flight of the imagination), the whole made terrible, if possible, by a very uncommon kind of blue lightning; the poor ship was very much pressed, yet doing what she could, shaking her sides, and groaning at every stroke. Sir Hyde on deck, lashed to windward! I soon lashed myself alongside of him, and told him the situation of things below, saying that the ship did not make more water than might be expected in such weather, and that I was only afraid of a gun breaking loose.

HMS Phoenix, *under the command of Captain Sir Hyde Parker, battles the seas of the Great Hurricane of 1780*

Archer found that the master's watch said it was five o'clock, though his own said it was a little after four. He was glad it was so near daylight 'and looked for it with much anxiety'. Then he exclaimed: 'Cuba, thou art much in our way!'

They were heading directly for the island's rocky southern shore, though it seemed they would sink in the heavy seas before she ran aground.

At this moment the pumps choked, and the weight of water began to drag the ship down. Even as Archer rounded up a party with axes to cut down the masts to lighten the ship and prevent her rolling so much, a huge wave, breaking directly across the ship smashed both the main and the mizzen [rear] masts and swamped the ship:

As soon as we could shake our heads above water, Sir Hyde exclaimed: "We are gone, at last, Archer, foundered at sea." "Yes, sir, farewell, and the Lord have mercy on us." I then turned about to look at

the ship; and thought she was struggling to get rid of some of the water; but all in vain, she was almost full below.

I then felt sorry that I could swim, as by that means I might be a quarter of an hour longer dying than a man who could not, and it is impossible to divest ourselves of a wish to preserve life. At the end of these reflections I thought I heard the ship thump and grinding under our feet; it was so. "Sir, the ship is ashore!" "What do you say?" "The ship is ashore, and we may save ourselves yet!" By this time the quarter-deck was full of men who had come up from below; and the Lord have mercy upon us, flying about from all quarters. The ship now made everybody sensible that she was ashore, for every stroke threatened the total dissolution of her whole frame; she found she was stern ashore, and the bow broke the sea a good deal, though it was washing clean over at every stroke. Sir Hyde cried out: "Keep to the quarter-deck, my lads, when she goes to pieces, it is your best chance."

Archer managed to get the foremast cut away so that the ship would not turn broadside to the waves, but five men were swept away in the process.

When it came, he found that there were mountainous seas on one side and mountainous rocks on the other. But the unmerciful sea had thrown the ship so high up the rocks she scarcely moved.

She was very strong, and did not go to pieces at the first thumping, though her decks tumbled in. We found afterwards that she had beat over a ledge of rocks, almost a quarter of a mile beyond us, where if she had struck, every soul of us must have perished.

Archer took off his coat and shoes, intending to swim for it, then looked around for a rope.

Luckily [I] could not find one, which gave me time for recollection: "This won't do for me, to be first man out of the ship, and first lieutenant; we may get to England again, and people will think I paid a great deal of attention to myself, and did not care for anybody else. No, that won't do; instead of being first, I'll see every man, sick and well, out of her before me."

The *Phoenix*, now somewhat sheltered from the worst of the raging sea, did hold together, and by noon the seamen had scrambled ashore, and had erected sailcloth tents, and brought ashore food and water – which was vital as there was no fresh water on that desolate part of the coast. After a good night's sleep, they were then faced by the prospect of being taken prisoner by the Spanish – England and Spain were still at war. If captured, they faced a three-hundred-mile forced march to Havana. Finding this prospect 'rather unpleasant', Archer suggested to Parker that he take the one remaining ship's boat, try to make it to Jamaica

and send back ships to pick the rest of them up. Parker agreed.

The next day they got the cutter ashore and the carpenters set to work. Two days later, at four in the afternoon, 'I embarked with four volunteers and a fortnight's provisions; hoisted the English colours as we put off from shore, and received three cheers from the lads left behind, and set sail with a light heart; having not the least doubt that, with God's assistance, we should come and bring them all off.'

It was a squally night, but clear enough to steer by the stars. In the morning they saw the coast of Jamaica, twelve leagues distant [1 league = 3 nautical miles, 3 ½ standard miles approx.], and at eight in the evening they arrived at Montego Bay. Four days later he returned to Cuba with a rescue party to find the ship's carpenters had built another boat, which would hold fifty, in case he had foundered. Two hundred and fifty men were taken off 'for some had died of the wounds they received in getting on shore; others of drinking rum and others had straggled into the country'.

The survivors arrived safely in Montego Bay, then were taken on to Port Royal where they 'were all honourably acquitted for the loss of the ship'. Archer was appointed the admiral's aide-de-camp. He was then made captain of the *Resource* and, after a successful rescue mission to St. Juan, captain of the *Tobago* – 'where I remain His Majesty's most true and faithful person and my dear mother's most dutiful son'.

Sole Survivor: the Wreck of the *Albion*

Such storms are not limited to the Caribbean. On 1 April 1822, the 447-ton *Albion* left New York with a crew of twenty-five and twenty-nine passengers on board. The weather was favourable and, after twenty days plain sailing, they made land at Fastnet. At 2 pm, they passed Cape Clear, but then the weather began to close in. There was a thick fog and heavy squalls blowing from the south. The crew shortened the sail, but at 4 pm the foreyard was carried away and the foretopsail split. As the gale increased they took in the mainsail and the mizzen topsail and set a small maintry sail.

The crew cleared the decks for nightfall. By eight the sea was throwing the ship on her beam ends. The huge waves carried away the mainmast completely and broke off the heads of the mizzen-mast and the foretopmast. The decks were swept clear of everything, including boats, the caboose house, bulwarks and compasses. The sea stove in all the hatches and the bulwarks. The staterooms and the main cabin filled with water. Six of the crew and one cabin passenger, Mr A.B. Convers of Troy, New York, were swept overboard. The *Albion's* first mate Henry Cammyer takes up the story:

The ship being unmanageable, and the sea making a complete breach over her, we were obliged to lash ourselves to the pumps, and being in total darkness, without correct compasses, could not tell how the ship's head lay. The axes being swept away, had not means of clearing the wreck. About one o'clock made the light of the Old Head of Kinsale, but could not ascertain how it bore; and at two found the ship embayed. The captain, anticipating our melancholy fate, called all the passengers up, who had not before been on deck. Many of them had received considerable injury when the sea first struck her, and were scarcely able to come on deck; others had been incessantly assisting at the pumps; and it is an interesting fact, that Miss Powell, an amiable young woman, who was on board, was desirous to be allowed to take her turn. One gentle-man, who had been extremely ill during the passage, Mr. William Everhart of Chester, Pennsylvania, was too feeble to crawl to the deck without assistance, but strange to say he was the only cabin passenger who was saved...'

At about 3 pm, the ship struck a reef. Half an hour later it broke in two. Twenty people clinging to the wreck, including Miss Powell and Mrs Pye, were swept away along with Captain John Williams who was trying to save them. The first mate and six of the crew then swam away from the wreck. Cammyer managed to reach a rock. In his exhausted state, he was washed off, but he managed to get back on it. His body and feet were badly bruised and he lay down on the rock, trying to gain the strength to climb the cliffs above him, which were almost vertical. While he lay there, a ship's steward and a passenger, Colonel Augustine J. Prevost, reached the rock, but were swept off and drowned. From his position on the rock, Cammyer described the scene of horror he saw back on the wreck:

Some of the passengers were suffocated on deck and in the fore rigging, and some must have been destroyed by an anchor which was loose on the fore-castle before the ship parted. It is scarcely possible to describe the devastation which followed. The entire cargo, consisting of cotton, rice, turpentine and beeswax, together with a quantity of silver and gold, to a large amount, was in all directions beaten to pieces by the severity of the sea, without possibility of saving it.

Cammyer and a few other shipmates managed to climb the cliffs and get help. Of the fifty-four on board, only nine survived. Local people took them into their homes and the next day they went to collect any bodies they could find. These were buried in Templetrine churchyard. Then Cammyer went to Kinsale where he met the US consul, who provided clothing for the survivors. Attempts were made to salvage the cargo and about five thousand pounds in coinage was raised.

As a seaman Cammyer knew what to expect. But the one cabin passenger who was saved, William Everhart of Chester, Pennsylvania, when he returned to American wrote his own account. The voyage had been pleasant enough, he said, though he himself had been very seasick and had been confined to his quarters. On 21 April, as they

A heavy swell builds up to storm force in the Bay of Biscay, seen from the deck of an Atlantic freighter

neared land, the passengers were in good spirits:

> *The storm of the day, it was supposed, was over; we were near to the coast, and all hands flattered themselves that they should reach their destined harbour; but, about nine o'clock in the evening, a heavy sea struck the ship, swept away several seamen from the deck, carried away her masts, and stove in her hatchways, so that every wave which passed over her, ran into her hold without anything to stop it – the railings were carried away, and the wheel which aided them to steer. In short, that fatal wave left the Albion a wreck. She was then about twenty miles from shore, and Captain Williams steadily and coolly gave his orders; he cheered the passengers and the crew with the hope that the wind would shift, and before morning blow off shore. The sea was very rough, and the vessel unmanageable; and the passengers were obliged to be tied to the pumps, that they might work them. All who could do no good on deck, retired below, but the water was knee deep in the cabin, and the furniture floating about, rendering the situation dangerous and dreadful.'*

But the wind did not change. All night long, the gale blew directly on shore, carrying the *Albion*

95

towards the rocks at the rate of about three miles an hour.

The complete hopelessness of the situation was known to few except Captain Williams. The coast was familiar to him; and he must have seen in despair and horror the certainty of our fate. At length, the ocean, dashing and roaring upon the precipice of rocks, told us that our hour had come. Captain Williams summoned all on deck, and briefly told them that the ship must soon strike; it was impossible to preserve her.

Everhart said that he was the last to leave the cabin but passenger Professor Fisher was left behind and perished below.

Some, particularly females, expressed their terror in wild shrieks. Major Gough, of the British army, remarked that "death, come as he would, was an unwelcome messenger, but that they must meet him like men". Very little was said by the others; the men awaited the expected shock in silence…

The deadly and relentless blast impelling them to destruction; the ship a wreck; the raging of the billows against the precipice, on which they were driving, sending back from the caverns and rocks, the hoarse and melancholy warnings of death, dark, cold and wet! In such a situation the stoutest heart must quake in utter despair. When there is a ray of hope, there may be a corresponding buoyancy of spirit. When there is anything to be done, the active man may drown the sense of danger while actively exerting himself; but here there was nothing to do but die! Just at the grey of dawn the Albion struck…

He noted that they could hardly have come ashore at a worse place. The Albion hit rocks at the foot of a near-vertical cliff.

Major Gough, of the British army, remarked that 'death, come as he would, was an unwelcome messenger, but that they must meet him like men'

The perpendicular precipice of rocks was nearly two hundred feet in height; the sea beating for ages against it has worn large caverns in its base, into which the waves rushed violently, sending back a deep and hollow sound, then, running out in various directions, formed whirlpools of great violence. For a perch [16.5 feet] or two from the precipice, rocks rise out of the water, broad at the bottom and sharp at the top; on one of these the Albion first struck, the next wave threw her further on the rock, the third further still, until she swung around, and her stern was driven against another, near in shore. In this situation, every wave making a complete breach over her, many were drowned on deck.'

A woman Everhart could not identify fell near him and cried for help. He let go of what he was holding on to and tried to pick her up, but another wave came, she was too exhausted to get up and drowned. At that time, Everhart reckoned, there were fifteen or sixteen corpses near of the ship.

The stern was now raised out of the water. It offered some protection from the waves, so Everhart made his way aft. Bales of cotton and the lighter items of cargo were floating about and being dashed against the rocks. The ship then broke in two and those in the bows drowned. Cammyer and others from the stern of the ship were clinging onto the rocks at the base of the cliff. Everhart managed to get a foothold on the rocks. Seeing him clamber on to the ledge Colonel Prevost said: 'Here is another poor fellow.'

The waves pounded them, sometimes sending spray fifty feet above their heads. One by one, the people clinging onto the rocks were swept away. One poor soul grabbed hold of Everhart's leg and nearly pulled him off. Weak and sick as he was, Everhart stood for several hours on one foot on a tiny crag, numb with cold.

As soon as it was light and the tide ebbed, people climbed down the rock and dropped him a rope. He tied it around his body and they hauled him to safety. Of the twenty-three cabin passengers, Everhart was the only survivor. He later remarked on the kindness of the local people.

'A sailor was drawn ashore naked, and one of the peasants took the shirt from his own back and put it on that of the sufferer.'

Everhart himself was taken to the mansion of James B. Gibbens, where he was bedridden for several weeks.

'They could not have treated me more tenderly, if I had been a brother,' he said.

News of the loss of the *Albion* spread throughout Europe and America and, when Everhart landed at Liverpool, he was mobbed, people were so eager to see the only passenger saved from the wreck of the *Albion*.

The Perils of the Fastnet

Gales in the area the *Albion* went down are still a peril for the modern mariner. In 1979, a storm blew up during the running of the biennial Fastnet Race. This starts at Cowes on the Isle of Wight. Competitors then head for the Fastnet Rock off southern Ireland, passing either north or south of the Isles of Scilly on the outbound leg. After rounding the Fastnet Rock they sail south of the Scillies back to Plymouth. The race has been held every two years since 1925. Until 1979, only one person had been killed – one man had been swept overboard in 1931. In 1979 the Fastnet race's near-perfect safety record would be devastated.

The race is always held in August. Usually the weather was good, but in 1957, 1958 and 1961 there had been gales. But the competitors considered that a good thing as it increased the boats' speeds.

In 1979, there were a record number of entrants – 303. On Saturday 11 August, they set off in fine calm weather. However, a depression was on its way. It had started out over Minnesota the day before. By Monday 13 August it had reached the mid-Atlantic and was moving fast. By that evening, it looked as if it would sweep northwards across Ireland. Instead, when it reached Ireland it stopped, for two fateful days.

At 3.05 pm on the 13th, the BBC broadcast a gale warning: 'Sole, Fastnet, Shannon, south-westerly gale force nine imminent.' Imminent usually means within six hours. At 11 pm the shipping forecast repeated the warning: 'Sole, severe gale force nine increasing storm force ten imminent. Fastnet, south-westerly gale force nine imminent, increasing storm force ten imminent. Shannon, north-westerly gale force nine increasing storm force ten imminent.' The storm was getting worse.

That night the Fastnet competitors were spread out over some twenty thousand square miles between the Scillies and Fastnet Rock. At 3 am on the morning of the 13th, a number of 'maydays' were received and three Irish and one English lifeboats took to the water. As the situation seemed set to get worse, at 3.16 am, the Land's End coastguard station called the Southern Rescue Coordination Centre at Plymouth for help at first light.

At 5.35 am a rescue helicopter took off from the Culdrose Naval Air Station in Cornwall. Another followed fifteen minutes later. These were joined by six more from other naval stations, and the RAF sent a helicopter and Nimrod patrol plane from Kinross in Scotland. With its sophisticated search equipment, the Nimrod took over as in-air commander of the operation, but the airwaves were so jammed with distress signals it was hard to get through to the overworked helicopters. Some crews flew mission after mission with barely half-an-hour's rest in between.

Lifeboats from thirteen stations were called out. Some were launched two or three times. They took off survivors and towed and escorted yachts into harbour. It took until 2 pm on 16 August until all the yachts had been accounted for.

On the 14th alone, seventeen yachts were abandoned. Crews and dead bodies were airlifted off. Other bodies were picked up from the sea. At 11.39 am, the crew members of the *Skullbladner* were plucked from a dinghy. And at 5.27 pm, the *Flash Light* was found adrift with no sign of her crew.

One of the yachts that had to be abandoned was the thirty-foot yacht *Grimalkin*. She was owned by David Sheahan, an accountant, who had done a great deal of sailing on smaller boats but had only recently bought an ocean-going vessel. Also on board were his seventeen-year-old son Matthew, Mike Doyle, Dick Wheeler and Nick Ward, who was epileptic. The navigator and second in command was Gerry Winks, who suffered from arthritis. They were hardly the fittest crew to take part in such an arduous race.

For the first two days, they were stuck in fog, with a heavy south-westerly swell making it an even more unpleasant voyage. When they heard the gale warning on Sunday afternoon, they rigged the yacht for a storm. At eight the next evening, they heard a French forecast warning of a force ten gale, gusting to storm force eleven. An hour later they were in the middle of the storm. Sailing under a storm jib only, the Grimalkin was rolling heavily, hurling things around the cabin. It was raining heavily. They tried to seal off the cabin, but with the decks awash, everything inside – food, clothing, bedding – was already soaked.

At 3 am on the 14th, they were on a port tack, still making for Fastnet. Nick Ward took the helm from Gerry Winks, who was exhausted and well on his way to hypothermia. With the sea still increasing, David Sheahan decided to abandon the race, turn and run before the wind. He threw a length of rope overboard as a makeshift sea anchor to try and steady her movement. The yacht was now surfing down the slopes of the waves and nearly somersaulting as she buried her bows in the trough.

All six crewmen now huddled in the cockpit with their safety harnesses hooked to lifelines that Sheahan had rigged before they left Cowes. Ward was at the helm, fighting for control. It was a losing battle. Between 3 am and 5 am, the *Grimalkin* found herself broadside to the waves six times. Each time she rolled over so far that the top of her masts touched the waves, throwing all six crewmen out of the cockpit and into the sea. Tethered by their harnesses they managed to scramble back into the boat, battered and bruised. On one occasion, Ward had to be dragged back by Sheahan, his leg badly damaged and probably broken.

David Sheahan managed to clamber back into the cabin and made a distress call. He was able to contact the *Mornington*, the escort yacht provided by the Royal Ocean Racing Club, which organises the Fastnet Race. She passed the signal to the coastguard station at Land's End. Meanwhile, on his way back to the cockpit, David Sheahan was knocked down and cut his head. Concussed, he lapsed in and out of consciousness.

The next time they were hit broadside by a wave, the *Grimalkin* turned over. David Sheahan was trapped under the cockpit. To free him, they had to release the tether of his safety harness. A minute or two later, the yacht righted itself, but they could not hold on to Sheahan, who drifted away.

The yacht had now been dismasted and the crew had to clamber through the rigging to get back to the cockpit. Ward had collapsed on the floor. Winks, who was unconscious, rolled on top of him. The two of them appeared to be dead. The rest of the crew pulled out a rubber dinghy and inflated it. Untethering their safety harnesses, they got on board and pushed themselves off, leaving Ward and Winks aboard.

An hour later, they were spotted by a Sea King helicopter. It hovered overhead and they were winched off one by one. After picking up two more survivors from the *Trophy*, the helicopter flew them back to Culdrose and safety.

The *Grimalkin* was still afloat and she had capsized again when Ward came around. He was underwater with his head being banged against the Fibreglass hull and his arms and legs tangled up in the rigging. He managed to extricate himself and, as the yacht righted itself again, clambered back into the cockpit. It was then that he noticed Winks being dragged through the water by his safety harness. Ward managed to wrap the tether around a winch and hauled him aboard. Amazingly, he was still alive. Ward gave him artificial respiration. He came around and said: 'If you see Margaret [his wife] again, tell her I love her.' Then he died.

Ward made for the cabin where he started bailing, but the sea was coming in too fast. He looked for the medicine for his epilepsy, which he was supposed to take every four hours. He could not find it and his next dose was well overdue. Then he heard an aeroplane overhead. He scrambled out, but it had gone. So he decided to return to the cockpit with his dead friend in case it returned. It was now four o'clock on Tuesday afternoon.

Soon after, a yacht appeared. Ward sounded the foghorn to attract her attention. The yacht fired off some distress rockets. Seeing these, a third yacht sent out a distress call. Eventually a helicopter turned up. An airman landed on the deck and winched Winks's body up. Then a harness was dropped for Ward and he was taken off. He was taken to Culdrose, then to Trelissick hospital in Truro. When Margaret Winks visited him there, he passed on her husband's dying message.

After he was released, Ward went to Baltimore in County Cork with Matthew Sheahan. The

Competitors in the ill-fated 1979 Fastnet race are winched to safety

Grimalkin had been found and towed there by a fishing boat. Undeterred, Ward and Sheahan got to work cleaning her up, ready to take her to sea again.

The US ambassador Kingman Brewster was to have been aboard the thirty-foot *Ariadne*, but he had been recalled to Washington for an urgent meeting. The yacht was skippered by sixty-one-year-old Frank Ferris, an American resident in Britain. Also on board was sixty-three-year-old American Robert Robbie. The rest of the crew were English – Bill LeFevre, David Crisp, nineteen-year-old medical student Matthew Hunt and

Rob Gilders, a sailmaker from the Caribbean.

Like the other boats, they rode out the heavy swell on the 13th. As the wind blew up at 11 pm, they shortened sail, but the mainsail split and had to be abandoned, effectively putting them out of the race. Nevertheless they continued with a small jib in the rapidly deteriorating conditions. When they heard the BBC's midnight shipping forecast, their anemometer was already reading sixty miles an hour. It was then they decided to give up.

They dared not make for Ireland as it was a lee shore. They needed to beat out to sea, but for the moment the best they could do was run before the wind. Then the jib split, so they rigged it as a sea anchor to try to hold them off the rocky coastline. The sea was now so heavy it rolled them right over. Crisp was trapped underneath, but managed to free himself. Gilders was thrown clear. When the yacht righted itself, the others pulled him back on board, while Crisp clambered on deck under his own steam.

During the roll, LeFevre had been hit on the head and was bleeding profusely. Hunt tended the wound but feared it might prove fatal. With the water in the cabin now up to their waists, the crew began bailing. Then a gust snapped the mast in two.

By dawn, they had managed to bail out the cabin, when she rolled over again, turning a complete 360 degrees. Robbie and Crisp, who were in the cockpit, were thrown overboard. Crisp was hauled back on board. But Robbie's harness snapped. He drifted away and there was nothing the other crewmen could do for him. They last saw him about fifty yards away. He waved before he disappeared forever.

It was then that they decided to abandon ship. Inflating a rubber dinghy, they climbed aboard,

They dared not make for Ireland as it was a lee shore. They needed to beat out to sea, but for the moment the best they could do was run before the wind

but this proved even more uncomfortable then the yacht. Its small canopy offered little shelter and they were forced to bail.

After two hours, they saw a ship and lit a red flare. The ship altered course, but before she could reach them the dinghy capsized. Crisp was trapped underneath, but freed himself and climbed back on board. Gilders had been thrown clear, but managed to struggle back after a few anxious moments.

The ship that had spotted them was a German freighter. She came alongside and lowered a rope ladder. Gilders jumped, caught the ladder and climbed up it to safety. Ferris jumped next. He missed the bottom rung of the ladder, fell in the water and, to everyone's horror, was swept away. His body was later recovered.

The freighter went around in an effort to get closer. Next it was Hunt's turn. He unhooked his safety harness and jumped for a higher rung of the rope ladder and scrambled up it. Moments later Crisp, now weakened, jumped for a lower rung. But he had forgotten to unhook the tether of his safety harness from the dinghy. He was halfway up the rope ladder when the dinghy pulled him away from the ship's side and jerked him off. Crisp and the dinghy, still with LeFevre in it, disappeared under the stern of the freighter and were probably hit by the propeller. They were never seen again. The freighter searched but, deciding they could not have survived, headed on up the Channel. At 1 am on the 15th the Lizard lifeboat took off Hunt and Gilders, the only survivors of a crew of six. In all, fifteen people died on the Fastnet Race that year, and only eighty-five of the 303 entrants completed the course. The winner was CNN boss Ted Turner in the sixty-one-foot yacht *Tenacious*.

Tsunami

Another peril of the sea is the tidal wave – or more accurately tsunami – caused by underwater earthquakes. These are common around Japan, particularly in the Gulf of Sagami, to the south of Tokyo, where a fault line runs underwater. On 23 December 1854, it moved, creating a disastrous tsunami. This was observed by two officers on the Russian frigate *Diana*.

The officer of the watch recorded:

We felt the first shock at 9.15 am. It was very strong and it went on for two or three minutes. At ten o'clock a huge wave rushed into the bay, and within a few minutes the whole town was underwater. The many ships at anchor were thrown against one another and seriously damaged. We immediately saw a great deal of debris floating. At the end of five minutes the water in the bay swelled and began boiling up, as if thousands of springs had suddenly broken out. The water was mixed with mud, straw and every kind of rubbish, and it hurled itself upon the town and the land to either side with shocking force. All the houses were wiped out. At 11.15 the frigate dragged her anchors and lost one of them. Presently she lost the other and the ship was then whirled around and swept along with a strength that grew greater with ever increasing speed of the water. At the same time thick clouds of vapour covered the site of the town and the air was filled with sulphurous exhalations. The rise and fall of the water in this narrow bay was such that it caused several whirlpools, among which the frigate spun round with such force that in the midst of these gyrations, she turned clear round forty-three times, but not without sustaining serious damage. Until noon the rising up and the falling of the water in the bay did not cease. The level varied from eight to forty feet in height. Towards two o'clock the bottom of the sea rose again, and so violently that several times the frigate was laid over and the anchor was seen in no more than four feet of water. At last the sea grew calm. The frigate floated in the middle of an inextricable tangle of

Safe and sound: rescued Fastnet competitors are taken back to dry land

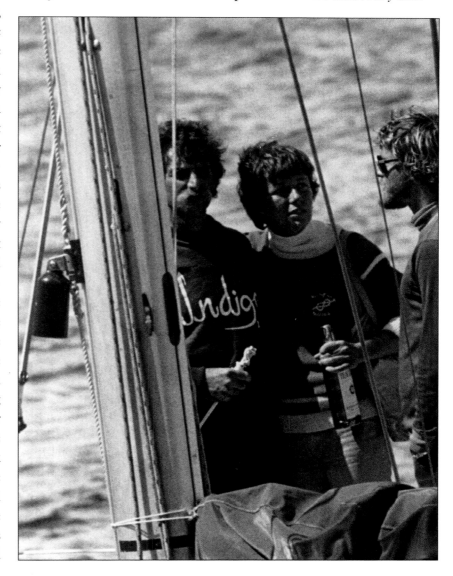

her own rigging and twisted chains. The bay was nothing more than an expanse of ruins.

Although ships out in the open sea rarely notice the passing of a tsunami, those at anchor in a confined body of water rarely survive, and the officers and men of the *Diana* were lucky to have made it through the tsunami's onslaught unscathed. They were luckier still not to have been ashore where over three thousand perished.

Tsunamis are not uncommon in the waters of northern Chile either. One had destroyed two Spanish galleons in Valdivia in 1575. Another had levelled Concepción in 1751. A third hit on 8 August 1868, when the USS *Wateree*, a two-masted single-stacked side-wheeler, was at anchor in the port of Arica in northern Chile. The *Wateree* survived, though she had been flung inland; she was moored next to Peruvian warship *America* and an American merchantman *Fredonia*, which were not so lucky. On board the *Wateree* was Lieutenant L.G. Billings who gave a startling account of the terrible fate of the other ships:

I was sitting in the cabin with the captain towards four o'clock in the afternoon when we gave a sudden start. The ship was trembling with the same vibration that occurs when the anchor is let go and the chains thunder in the hawseholes. We knew that it could be that, and we ran on deck. Our eyes were at once caught by a huge cloud of dust over the land, which was coming up from the southeast while the terrible thundering grew louder and louder. As we watched, stupefied, the hills seemed to be capsizing, and the ground moved like short choppy waves of a rough sea. The cloud swallowed up Arica. In that very instant, through its impenetrable veil, there arose shrieks for help, the din of falling houses, and the thousand mixed noises of a great calamity. Meanwhile, our ship was shaken as if by the grasp of a gigantic hand. Then the cloud passed on.

As the dust thinned out we rubbed our eyes and stared, unable to believe what we saw: where a few seconds before there had stood a happy prosperous city, busy, active, and full of life, we saw nothing but ruins. The less seriously wounded of the unhappy people caught under the wreckage of what had been their houses were struggling among the ruins, and everywhere shrieks, cries of pain, and calls for help tore the air under the pitiless sun shining in a cloudless sky.

We were worried about the coming of a tsunami, and we put out to sea; but the water was calm and unruffled, and it might have been supposed that the four or five minutes that we had just passed through as well as the shockingly distressing scene upon which for the moment we were turning our backs were part of a nightmare. Nevertheless, as a measure of prudence the captain set out extra anchors, had the hatches closed, the guns lashed and lifelines rigged.

Responding to the pitiful cries of survivors on the shore, the *Wateree's* crew were preparing to launch the ship's boats when:

when all at once a hoarse murmuring noise made us look up. Looking towards the land we saw, to our horror, that where a moment before there had been a jetty, all black with human beings, there was nothing. Everything had been swallowed in a moment by the sudden rising of the sea, which the ship, floating upon it, had not noticed. At the same time we saw the yawl and its sailor carried away by the irresistible wave towards the lofty, vertical cliff of the Morro, where they disappeared in the foam as the wave broke against the rock. At that very instant there was another earthquake shock, accompanied by a terrible roaring on the land that went on for several minutes. Once more we saw the ground move in waves and go from left to right, and this time the sea drew back from the land until we were stranded and the bottom of the sea was exposed, so that we saw what had never been seen before, fish struggling on the seabed and the monsters of the deep aground. The round-hulled ships rolled over on their sides, while our Wateree sat down upon her flat bottom; and when the sea

Artwork of the steamship La Plata, *caught in a tsunami that hit the island of St. Thomas, West Indies, on 18 November 1867. The wave measured upwards of 60 feet*

came back, returning not as a wave, but rather as a huge tide, it made our unhappy companions turn turtle, whereas the Wateree rose unhurt on the churning water. From that moment on, the sea seemed to defy all natural laws. Currents rushed in opposite directions, dragging us along at a speed that we could never have reached even if we had been going at full steam. The earth was still quaking at irregular intervals, but less violently and for shorter periods each time.

The Peruvian ironclad America, which was held to be one of the fastest ships in the world at the time, was still afloat, and so was the American ship Fredonia. The America, who had tried to get out to sea with her engines running at full speed before the withdrawal of the water, was nevertheless partially stranded, and her hull was stove in. Now the sea was carrying her at a great speed towards the shore, and her funnels belching thick clouds of smoke she seemed to be running in to the assistance of the helpless Fredonia, which was being drawn towards the cliffs of the Morro. Captain Dyer of the Fredonia, believing this to be the case, ran aft and hailed the man-of-war, which was now no more than a few yards away. "Ahoy! You can do nothing for us, our bottom is smashed in. Save yourselves! Goodbye!" A moment later the Fredonia broke to pieces against the cliff and not a man was saved, while a counter-current miraculously took hold of the Peruvian ship and carried her in the other direction.

The last rays of the sun were lighting up the Andes when we saw to our horror that the tombs in which the former inhabitants had buried their dead, in the slopes of the mountain, had opened, and in concentric rings, as in an amphitheatre, the mummies of natives dead and forgotten for centuries appeared on the surface. They had been buried sitting up, facing the sea. The nitre-impregnated soil had preserved them astonishingly, and the violent shocks that had crumbled the desert-dry earth now uncovered the horrifying city of the dead, buried long ago.

Words cannot convey the appalling appearance of the scene. Our minds had been much worked upon by what we had undergone already and we were ready to believe that the Day of Judgement had come and that the world was going to disappear. The bitterness of so terrifying a death went beyond anything that we could imagine.

It had been dark for some time when the lookout hailed the deck and said that a breaking wave was coming. Staring into the night we first made out a thin phosphorescent line which, like a strange kind of mirage, seemed to be rising higher and higher in the air: its crest, topped by the baleful light of that phosphorescent glitter, showed frightful masses of black water below. Heralded by the thunder of thousands of breakers all crashing together, the tidal wave that we had dreaded for hours was at last upon us.

Of all the horrors, this seemed the worst. We were chained to the bed of the sea, powerless to escape. We had taken all the precautions that were humanly possible, and now we could do nothing but watch this monstrous wave approach, without the moral support of having something to do or the hope that the ship could go through the mass of water rushing to overwhelm us. We could only hold on to the rails and wait for the catastrophe.

With a terrifying din, our ship was engulfed, buried under a half-liquid, half-solid mass of sand and water. We stayed under for a suffocating eternity. Then, groaning in all her timbers, our solid old Wateree pushed her way to the surface, with her gasping crew still hanging on to the rails. A few men were seriously hurt. None was killed and nobody was missing. It was a miracle that I can scarcely really believe in even at this length of time. Our survival was certainly due to the construction of the ship, her shape, and her fitting out, which allowed the water to pour off the deck almost as quickly as if she had been a raft.

The ship had been carried along at a very great speed, but all at once she became motionless. In the end, after a short wait, we lowered the lantern over the side and we discovered that we had run aground. Where we were we could not tell. There were still a few waves that came to strike us, but they were not so strong, and presently they stopped altogether. For some time we stayed at our posts, but as the ship remained quite still and nothing further happened the order was given for the exhausted crew to go below and sleep in their hammocks.

The sun rose upon such a spectacle of desolation as can rarely have been seen. We were high and dry, three miles from our anchorage and two miles inland. The wave had carried us at an unbelievable speed over the sand dunes which line the shore, across a valley, and beyond the railway line that

The USS Wateree, *left high and dry by a tsunami which struck the northern Chilean port of Arica on 8 August 1868*

goes to Bolivia, leaving us at the foot of the coastal range of the cordillera of the Andes. Upon an almost vertical cliff we found the mark that the tidal wave had left: it was forty-seven feet up. If the wave had carried us for another sixty yards, it would have smashed us against the perpendicular mountain wall.

Near us there lay the wreck of the English three-master, the Channacelia; one of her anchor chains was wrapped around her as many times as its length would allow, thus showing how the vessel had rolled over and over, head over heels. Some way further off, nearer the sea, lay the ironclad America upon her side, quite wrecked.

Nothing was left of Arica. Even the ruins were hidden under a flat plain of sand which covered everything except the outlying regions, where the wave had deposited a huge number of corpses. Billings also reported the strange sight of a dead woman seated on a dead horse in a crevasse. He

presumed that the fissure had opened up beneath them as they were fleeing.

Of the city's ten or fifteen thousand inhabitants, only a few hundred survived. They waited for help for three weeks, surviving on food and drinking water from the *Wateree*. Eventually the US navy frigate Powhatan arrived with more supplies. In all, it is thought that the Chilean earthquake and tsunami of 1868 took 25,000 lives.

'Freak' Waves

On 3 June 1984, the sail-training ship *Marques* was weathering a storm off Bermuda. After fourteen hours it seemed to be blowing itself out and most of the crew members were sleeping peacefully below. Then twenty-two-year-old helmsman Philip Sefton suddenly saw a 'freakish wave of incredible force and size'. It slammed into the ship, knocking her on her side. Water poured in

Another view of the grounded Wateree, *which survived the tsunami intact, showing the* America *in the background*

through the open hatchways and in forty-five seconds she had sunk. Of the twenty-eight on board the *Marques* there were just nine survivors.

Although mariners had long talked about such giant waves, they were long thought to be a myth. On average the world's oceans claim one ship a week, often in mysterious circumstances. Usually human error or poor maintenance is blamed. However, sometimes top class crews in world-class vessels with unblemished track records go down. This was the case in 1978 when the state-of-the-art cargo ship *München* disappeared. She was on a perfectly routine crossing of the Atlantic when, at 3 am on 12 December, she sent out a garbled mayday message from the mid-Atlantic. Over a hundred ships began combing the ocean. They hoped to find a life raft at least. They found not a living soul.

The *München* was never found. She went down with all twenty-seven hands. However, a few bits of wreckage were found after an exhaustive search. These included an unlaunched lifeboat which bore a vital clue. One of its attachment pins was twisted

as if an extreme force had hit it, yet the lifeboat had been stowed sixty-six feet above the water line.

In a storm, waves often reach a height of forty feet. Oceanographers and meteorologists say that fifty-foot waves occur occasionally. This is the highest wave that marine architects build ships to withstand. It is theoretically possible for waves of a hundred feet to occur, but this should happen only once in ten thousand years. However, it has now been discovered that huge waves do occur much more frequently than that. On New Year's Day 1985, an eighty-five-foot wave hit the *Draupner* oil rig off Norway. And since 1990, twenty vessels have reported being struck by waves of this size off the coast of South Africa. When oceanographer Marten Grundlingh looked into this he found that all the ships had been at the edge of the Agulhas Current, where warm Indian Ocean water meets the colder Atlantic flow. Satellite radar surveillance confirmed that wave height at the edge of this current could grow to gigantic proportions, if the wind direction opposed the current flow.

However, this did not explain the wave that hit the *Draupner* or what happened to the *München* that had sunk way out in the middle of the Atlantic.

Then in March 2001 there were two near disastrous wave strikes far away from such troublesome currents. The cruise liner *Bremen* was carrying 137 German tourists in Antarctic waters when she was hit by a huge wall of water. The impact knocked out her power, leaving her helpless in a huge sea. Unable to keep her into the waves, there was a real risk the ship would capsize. None of the passengers would survive for long in lifeboats in such freezing conditions. Fortunately, working with emergency power only, the crew managed to restart the engines.

A few days later, another Antarctic cruise ship was nearly swamped. At 5 am on 2 March the *Caledonian Star*'s first officer saw a huge wave over twice the height of the others bearing down on them.

'The ship went down like freefall,' he said.

More than a hundred feet high, the wave rolled over the ship, flooding the bridge and smashing much of the navigation and communication equipment. However, the engines kept running and the *Caledonian Star* limped to port.

Examining data from the *Draupner* oil rig, scientists now concede that hundred-foot waves can exist. They feed off the energy of the waves around them until they reach the height of an office block. And freak waves are not just far bigger, they are so steep they are almost breaking, presenting a near-vertical wall of water that is almost impossible to ride over. The wave breaks over the ship, no matter her size, swamping her.

While a fifty-foot wave hits a ship with a force of fifteen tons a square metre, a hundred-footer hits with an impact of a hundred tons a square metre. It is now thought that such a giant sank the freighter *München* without leaving any trace.

The München *meets her doom in this image from the BBC Horizon progamme Freak Wave* (Image courtesy of the BBC)

8 Ferry Disasters

If the perils of storms, waves and piracy were not bad enough, the age of steam brought with it a new danger – the boiler explosion. Particularly at risk were the steamboats that ferried people and goods up and down the Mississippi River.

On the morning of 24 February 1830, one of these Mississippi riverboats, the *Helen McGregor*, stopped in at Memphis. It stopped there for three-quarters of an hour. One of the passengers went ashore to conduct some business. When he returned, he found a great crowd of people standing on the boiler deck – that is, the part of the upper deck that extends directly over the boilers. It 'presented one dense mass of human bodies,' he said. He estimated that there were between four hundred and five hundred people on board. The passenger then went to have his breakfast on one of the long tables that could accommodate all sixty of the cabin passengers.

'I had almost finished my breakfast, when the pilot rung his bell for the engineer to put the machinery in motion,' he recalled. 'The boat having just shoved off, I was in the act of raising my cup to my lips, the tingling of the pilot bell yet on my ear, when I heard an explosion resembling the discharge of a small piece of artillery. The report was perhaps louder than usual in such cases; for an exclamation was half uttered by me, that the gun was well loaded, when the rushing sound of steam and the rattling of glass in some of the cabin windows checked my speech and told me what had occurred. I almost involuntarily bent my head and body down to the floor – a vague idea seemed to shoot through my mind that more than one boiler might burst and that by assuming this position the destroying matter would pass over without touching me.

'The general cry of "a boiler has burst" resounded from one end of the table to the other; and, as if by a simultaneous movement, all started on their feet. Then commenced a general race to the ladies' cabin, which lay more towards the stern of the boat. All regard to order of deference to sex seemed to be lost in the struggle for which should be first and furthest removed from the dreaded boilers.'

But our passenger was made of sterner stuff.

'The danger had already passed. I remained standing by the chair on which I had previously been sitting. Only one or two persons stayed in the cabin with me. As yet no more than half-a-minute had elapsed since the explosion…'

However, he was full of admiration for the ladies who 'exhibited a degree of firmness worthy of all praise. No screaming, no fainting – their fears, when uttered, were not for themselves, but for their husbands and children.'

The niceties observed, now the situation had to be taken in hand.

'I advanced from my position to one of the cabin doors for the purpose of enquiring who were injured, when, just as I reached it, a man entered the opposite one, both his hands covering his face and exclaiming, "Oh God! Oh God! I am ruined!" He immediately began to tear off his clothes. When stripped, he presented the most shocking spectacle: his face was entirely black – his body without a particle of skin. He had been flayed alive.'

A mattress was brought from one of the cabins. He was laid on it and covered with a blanket. The passenger took his name and address. He talked of his wife and children, and how hard it was to die without bidding them farewell. Oil and cotton were applied to his wounds, but soon 'he became insensible to earthly misery'.

'Before I had done attending to him, the whole floor of the cabin was covered with unfortunate sufferers. Some bore up under the horrors of their situation with a degree of resolution amounting to heroism. Others were wholly overcome by the sense of pain, the suddenness of the disaster, and the near approach of death…

'To add to the confusion, persons were every moment running about to learn the fate of their friends and relatives – fathers, sons, brothers – for in this scene of unmixed calamity, it was impossible to say who were safe, or who had perished. The countenances of many were so much disfigured as to be past recognition.'

Our passenger was drawn to a man who lay unnoticed on the floor a little distance from the rest. He was not burnt or scalded, but one of his thighs was broken. The bone had severed an artery, which was gushing blood.

'He betrayed no displeasure at the apparent neglect with which he was treated – he was perfectly calm. I spoke to him and he said he was very weak, but felt himself going – it would soon be over.'

Someone fetched a doctor who said that he could be saved if they amputated his leg. They would have to get him ashore first but the steamer was out from the bank and it took sometime for boats to reach it. The man was taken ashore and his leg was amputated, but he died soon after.

There were more corpses in the boiler room, which was a picture of utter destruction.

'On the starboard wheel-house lay a human body, in which life was not yet extinct, though apparently there was no sensibility remaining. The body must have been thrown from the boiler deck, a distance of thirty feet. Tufts of hair, shreds of clothing and splotches of blood might be seen in every direction. A piece of skin was picked up by a gentleman on board, which appeared to have been peeled off by the force of the steam. It extended from the middle of the arm down to the tips of the fingers, the nails adhering to it. So dreadful had been the force that not a particle of flesh adhered to it. The most skilful operator could scarcely have effected such a result.'

Several died from inhaling steam or gas, though they appeared quite uninjured. The number killed was never ascertained. Many had been flung into the water and never rose again. The rescue operation was so disorderly that the survivors were not kept together. No list of their names could be gathered to compare to the passenger manifest.

It is known that the captain died instantly in the explosion. Later the engineer, who had survived, explained what had happened. At Memphis the steamer had grounded raising its starboard, causing the water on board to run into the port boiler. The fires were stoked before they left, overheating the empty starboard boiler and cracking its head. When they pulled away and the steamer returned to an even keel, water ran from the port boiler back into the overheated starboard boiler, turned instantly to steam and the pressure blew off the cracked head.

The passenger also discovered how he and the other cabin passengers had been spared. Between the boiler room and the cabin where they had been seated, there was an iron post.

'The boiler head was in point blank range with

The pleasure boat Eastland *where she rolled over and sank on the Chicago River, 24 July 1915, with a loss of 844 lives*

the breakfast table in the cabin; and had it not been obstructed by the iron post, must have made a clean sweep of those seated at the table.'

It had penetrated the post to the depth of an inch, ricocheted off at an angle and buried itself in a bale of cotton.

Tragedy on the Chicago River

One of most notorious shipwrecks in US history occurred when the excursion steamer *Eastland* slowly rolled over while she was still moored to her dock between LaSalle and Clark Streets on the south bank of the Chicago River. It was 7.28 am and there were 2,572 passengers on board. They were largely Western Electric employees and their families and friends who were going to an annual company picnic in Michigan City, Indiana. In the accident, 844 perished – making the tragedy Chicago's single most deadly disaster.

The causes of the disaster are still subject to debate, but several facts are clear. The steamer had a reputation for being top-heavy and had at several times in the past been reported as listing in an

alarming way. Her water-ballasting system was already seen as dangerously unstable. A series of modifications had steadily increased the top-heavy tendency of the vessel. Fearful of just such a disaster that eventually overtook the *Eastland*, more lifeboats had been added, increasing her instability.

All these changes made her so unsteady that with a full passenger load of 2,500 persons she could be kept upright only through exceptional seamanship. The owners, captain and engineers were apparently not aware of the dangers posed by her instability and did not compensate with added ballast. Thus she turned turtle the first time a full passenger load was taken aboard after her last modification. Ironically, the fatal addition was those extra lifeboats.

Lawsuits continued for more than twenty years. The *Eastland* herself was refloated, renamed the *Wilimette* and reassigned as a naval training vessel until she was broken up for scrap in 1947.

The worst ferry disaster in history happened in the early hours of 21 December 1987, when the ferry *Doña Paz*, bound from Tacloban on the island of Leyte in the Philippines to the capital

Manila on Luzon, collided with the tanker *Vector*. Both ships sank within minutes near Bantayan Island, about three hundred miles southeast of Manila. The *Doña Paz* was only supposed to carry 1,550 people, but in the run-up to Christmas many more were on board.

A passing ship picked up 189 people. Three navy ships were sent, along with air force rescue helicopters. But she had sunk at around 5 am and the darkness hampered the rescue. In all over 4,300 perished.

The *Princess Victoria*

In Europe there has been a series of disasters with car ferries. This is because their open car decks have no watertight doors. Water can spread across them unimpeded and as they flood they make the vessel dangerously unstable. An open car deck was to prove lethal on 30 January 1953, when the British Railways ferry *Princess Victoria* sailed from Stranraer for the port of Larne, some sixteen miles northeast of Belfast.

It was a rough night. The seven-thousand-ton motor vessel *Clan MacQuarrie* had been blown on to rocks ten miles off the Butt of Lewis and a Fleetwood trawler, the *Michael Griffith*, had gone down nine miles south of Barra Head.

From Stranraer, the *Princess Victoria* sailed up the loch and out into the open sea for the short crossing to Ireland. Even before she cleared Milleur Point at the head of the peninsula to the west, she was making heavy weather of it, her bow burying itself in the churning sea and the stern lifting the screws out of the water. Visibility was also restricted by heavy snow.

About four miles out from Milleur Port, Captain James Ferguson thought better of it and attempted to turn back to Stranraer. This brought the stern doors, which had been damaged the year before, around to face the heavy sea. The battering forced them open and sea water began to pour in. Attempts were made to close them, but the doors were buckled and nothing could be done. Captain Ferguson radioed for help.

Unable to get back into the loch, Ferguson made a dash for the shelter of the Irish coast, twenty-five miles away. Meanwhile the passengers were asked to put on their life jackets. The water on board slopped about the car deck, making her unstable, and drained through the scuppers into the engine room. Soon the engine room was ankle deep in water. The pumps were working overtime and the *Princess Victoria* was listing to starboard. An SOS was sent, but in the appalling conditions the lifeboat and other search vessels could not find her.

Ferguson actually made it into the shelter of Belfast Lough before the ship foundered. Ferguson was loath to order 'abandon ship' in winds that gusted to eighty miles an hour but when the ship was on her beam ends, he had no choice. The starboard was so low in the water that it was almost impossible to launch the lifeboats. One got away with just six men aboard. Another, full of women and children, was capsized by a wave. Two more were overturned when the *Princess Victoria* turned turtle. Some of the passengers and crew found a brief refuge on her

British Railways ferry Princess Victoria. *As with many ferry sinkings, her doors played a major role in the tragedy*

upturned hull. But it soon became clear that she was settling and they had to swim for life rafts. In the churning seas few made it. Eventually when the coastal freighter *Orchy* came upon them, it was no easy task to pluck the survivors from the raging sea. Some were hauled on board with boat hooks only to be found dead when they reached the deck. Of the 174 men, women and children on board the *Princess Victoria* only forty-one were rescued.

A court of enquiry found British Railways to blame. After the accident in which the stern doors had been damaged the previous year, the car deck had flooded and British Rail had been told to make the scuppers bigger so that it could drain. They had failed to do so, in the words of Captain Morrow, an assistant manager of British Railways, because of the 'inconvenience suffered by ladies with fancy shoes and nylon stockings'.

The Sinking of the *Zenobia*

In 1978, a new ro-ro design came out of the Kockums shipyard in Malmo for use in the Mediterranean and the Great Lakes. The new ships were 540 feet long and 75.5 feet wide, and again had an open deck for vehicles. In February 1980, one of these ferries, belonging to the Swedish Nordo Shipping Company, called the *Zenobia*, was plying between Patras in Greece and Tartous in Syria when she was hit by a freak wave, causing her to heel thirty-five degrees to starboard. She was righting herself when another wave rolled her back to forty degrees where she stayed. The rolling had snapped the lashing on about forty lorries and the load had shifted. An adjustment of ballast and fuel brought her back onto an even keel, but the lorry drivers insisted that she put in to the nearby port of Volvos. It was a taste of worse things to come.

On 30 May 1980, the *Zenobia* left Koper in what was then Yugoslavia bound for Tartous. On board were a crew of thirty and 121 passengers. There were 135 vehicles on board, mostly lorries, weighing in total around 4,000 tons. Shortly after midnight on 2 June, when she was about ten miles south of Cape Dolos on Cyprus, the steering mechanism seems to have malfunctioned. She began to sheer to starboard. To counteract this, the helmsman turned to port. She then heeled to port and, within three seconds, came to rest at forty degrees. This lifted the starboard screw out of the water and the engines shut down.

The captain gave orders to prepare to abandon ship. Meanwhile the chief engineer tried to pump ballast to right the list. Below they found that sea water taken on board to cool the engines was being discharged onto the vehicle deck, rather than back into the sea. From there it cascaded down into the engine room. Soon on the port side, the water was around twelve feet deep.

It was now impossible to take on ballast as the intake to the starboard tanks was above sea level. They tried to shift the fuel, but the oil was cold and viscous and would not pump easily. The fire hoses were rigged to fill the starboard tank, but the intake for the fire pump was also out of the water.

At half-past-midnight, the captain sent out a mayday. The German freighter *Ville de Levan* turned up at 1.30 am and began taking off the passengers. A Russian ship arrived a quarter of an hour later to assist. A tug called the *Onisillos* arrived from Limassol at 7.30, but refused to tie up alongside because of the *Zenobia's* heavy list. However, she did pass over a hose to fill the starboard tank. When this parted, the tug towed the crippled ferry into Larnaca Bay to pump on ballast in the sheltered waters there. But when they arrived the port authorities refused to allow the *Onisillos* to do the pumping, ruling that a tug from Larnaca must be used. It would arrive the following morning.

The *Mercantino Brigadino* duly arrived and spent the whole day pumping on ballast – to no effect. The *Zenobia* was still shipping water on the port side and the generator powering the pumps overheated. Then the Greek salvage tug *Vernicos Dimitrios* turned up, but she could not get to work because of competing salvage claims. When these were sorted out, she began pumping at about 1.30 on the morning of 5 June. By 6 am one of the starboard tanks was full and the list reduced to thirty-two degrees. But the water was leaking out. It was then discovered that the valve connecting the ballast tanks had been left open and the water that had been pumped into the starboard tank was leaking into the port tank. When that was closed, they began filling another starboard tank and by 12.30 pm the list had been reduced to thirty degrees.

The danger now seemed to be over. The crew went on board to work on the ferry's main engine and the salvage tug left. The generators were repaired and the water in the engine room and vehicle deck had been pumped out. Then she began to list between two and three degrees to starboard. Ballast was pumped to port to counteract this. But no one seems to have read this as a warning that the ship was now dangerously unstable.

Shortly before midnight, she flopped to port about ten degrees. Then the list increased to twenty. The ship was now low in the water, which poured in. At 12.20 am, the captain gave the order to abandon ship. The crew went aboard the *Mercanto Brigadino* and the captain asked master of the tug to tow the sinking ship into shallower water. He refused, saying that he needed permission from the supreme court of Cyprus. They tried to reach the port authorities by radio, but failed. So they raced into the port and at one o'clock received permission to tow the ship into shallow water. As there was no power on the *Zenobia* to raise the anchor and the *Mercanto Brigadino* had nothing with which to cut the cable, suitable equipment would have to be transferred from the *Vernicos Dimitrios*.

At 1.55 am, the tug arrived back to where they had left the *Zenobia* only to find a patch of floating debris. She had sunk in twenty fathoms where she still lies, complete with a full cargo, including lorries, and even, allegedly, the captain's own car!

The *Herald of Free Enterprise*

On 6 March 1987, the *Herald of Free Enterprise* was leaving Zeebrugge for Dover with 460 passengers on board. Unbeknown to them, there was a problem with this type of vessel. Three years earlier, the *Herald of Free Enterprise's* sister ship, the *Pride of Free Enterprise*, had sailed from Dover with both her bow and stern doors open because the assistant bosun had fallen asleep. Over the next year, the *Pride* sailed twice more with either the bow or stern door open. Her captain even wrote to the company's managing director suggesting that an indicator light be installed on the bridge, showing whether the doors were open or closed. When the matter was discussed, the deputy superintendent said: 'Do they need an indicator light to tell them whether the deck storekeeper is awake and sober?'

Although all the masters of ships of the *Herald's* design agreed that indicator lights should be installed, the management decided that discipline was the answer.

On the evening of 6 March, the crew members of the *Herald* were tired. Eighty per cent of them were working twenty-four hour shifts, making two round trips across the Channel, and they were now embarking on the return leg of the second trip. Zeebrugge as a port had a slow turnaround time, as it was necessary to pump water ballast into ferries' bows to lower their main vehicle decks to the height of the loading ramp.

At 7 pm, the bosun's assistant Mark Stanley, the man whose job it was to close the bow doors, was asleep in his cabin. He did not hear harbour stations being sounded – his cue to close the doors. Chief Officer Leslie Sabel was also tired as he made his rounds. He saw a man in orange overalls who he took to be Mark Stanley, assumed that the bow doors had been closed and returned to the bridge to report that they were ready to sail.

The passengers were relaxing in the cafeteria or in the cabins below decks when the *Herald* pulled away from the pier. At 7.20, she passed out of the inner breakwater and into the shipping channel. Captain Lewry then dismissed the second officer and told Chief Officer Sabel to take his dinner break.

The *Herald* was now heading out into the Channel with her bows three feet lower than usual, and her bow doors open to the sea. As she reached fifteen knots, water began pouring in through the bow doors and as she filled, the bows dropped, increasing the flow of water. Soon water was pouring in at a rate of two hundred tons a minute. A steward on H deck heard the water and assumed that a pipe had burst. He called the assistant purser who put out a call on the ship's public address system summoning the ship's carpenter. This was code for a general alarm, so as not to panic the passengers.

At 7.27, the helmsman reported that she would not respond. Lewry slammed the engines into reverse, but it was too late. She was already listing thirty degrees to port and forty seconds later, she rolled over and settled on her side on the bottom.

Passengers in the cafeteria were only alerted when things started sliding off their tables. Some started screaming. The lights went out and soon they were chest deep in water.

> **Although all the masters of ships of the *Herald's* design agreed that indicator lights should be installed, the management decided that discipline was the answer**

As the ship rolled over Mark Stanley was thrown out of his bunk. He ran to the lifeboats, grabbed an axe and began smashing the windows of the passenger lounge so people could get out. But the passengers were thirty feet below. Stanley grabbed a rope and lowered it, then climbing down, he reassured the passengers that help was on its way. He climbed up again, told two soldiers who were on their way home on leave to get a ladder, then he passed out due to his dip in the cold water. He was covered with an overcoat and taken to safety.

At 7.36, the captain of the dredger *Sanderas* spotted the *Herald* on her side and called the port authorities. Immediately, their harbour rescue plan went into operation. Within minutes, the *Herald* was surrounded by tugs and a helicopter dropped a team of divers. Their leader Lieutenant- Commander Guy Couwenbergh dived into the passenger lounge where he found himself surrounded by people weak from exposure to the thirty-seven-degree water. The ladder the soldiers had brought was too short, so Couwenbergh told the other divers to get some rope. When it was lowered he tied it around one of the passengers who was then hauled up.

Taking the passengers out one by one this way was a laborious business. For some of them, when their time came, it would be too late. To Couwenbergh fell the thankless task of selecting who should go first.

More windows were smashed and other ropes lowered, but many of those in the water were too weak to climb up and one woman fell off. A wicker basket was found to haul the children up.

The Herald of Free Enterprise *in Zeebrugge harbour where she capsized on 6 March 1987*

The Herald of Free Enterprise *today, raised and working again in India*

That night 188 people perished on the *Herald of Free Enterprise*; 350 survived. A board of enquiry established that although the immediate cause of the disaster was the failure to close the bow doors, the real cause lay with an indifferent, incompetent Board of Directors, who 'did not apply their minds to the question: What orders should be given for the safety of our ships?'. Indicator lights have now been installed on similar ships.

Even that, however, did not stop the sinkings of ro-ro ferries. On the night of 28 September 1994, the Swedish-owned *Estonia* was sailing from Tallinn in Estonia to Stockholm, Sweden, when waves ripped off its visor-style bow door and water poured onto the vehicle deck.

The ship capsized and sank off the Finnish coast in Europe's worst maritime disaster since the sinking of the *Wilhelm Gustloff*. Most of the passengers were trapped inside. In all, 852 people died, including ninety-four who managed to leave the vessel but died of exposure in freezing water. Only 137 people survived the disaster. The cause was a design fault that prevented the bow door closing properly.

Meanwhile the captain of the Sea Horse rammed the bow of his tug against the *Herald's* stern so that people could jump on board.

The dead found inside the wreck were laid out under blankets on the *Herald's* side. Most had died from hypothermia. Miraculously, when checked for signs of life, two of them were found still to be living and they were rushed ashore.

Four lorry drivers who had been asleep in cabins in the bowels of the ship, awoke to find themselves trapped. Two of them were badly injured. One of them fell in the water and drowned. The rest began banging on a bulkhead. Soon their bangs were answered and two of the drivers were rescued.

Meanwhile, overcrowded passenger ferries continued to sink in the Third World. On 29 August 2002 the ferry *Joola* sank off Dakar in Senegal, killing most of those on board. All the passengers raced to one side of the overcrowded ferry to take cover during a storm, causing it to capsize. The authorities said 970 of the 1,034 people on board died, but the death toll is likely much higher, as children under five did not have tickets and would not have been counted on the passenger lists. Only sixty-four of the passengers survived.

The *Joola* was built to carry a maximum of six hundred people. On 29 August, at least five hundred were crowded onto the top deck alone for the sixteen-hour journey from Ziguinchor to Dakar, the capital. Some men were carrying everything they possessed in the world on their backs, while women were laden with mangoes and palm oil which they aimed to sell in Dakar. And, as it was the low season for tourists, there were few cars in the ferry's hold to help stabilise her.

When the ferry rode into a storm, the people on the top deck were hit with wind and rain coming from starboard. To get under cover, they moved en masse to port. That movement caused a fatal shift in the ferry's centre of gravity and the ship turned turtle. At the time, she was eleven hours' sailing time from shore when, as a coastal ferry, she was only permitted to sail six hours from shore.

Senegal's president, Abdoulaye Wade, declared three days of national mourning, and an official said: 'Senegal is only a small country. More than a thousand people died, and everyone knows someone who knows someone. We are all affected by something like this.'

President Wade later acknowledged his government's 'obvious' responsibility for the disaster and he accepted the resignations of his transport minister, Youssouph Sakho and armed forces minister, Youba Sambou, in connection with the sinking.

The Sinking of the *Wahine*

At 8.40 pm on 9 April, 1968, the Union Steam Ship ferry *Wahine* left Lyttleton Harbour on the South Island of New Zealand on her regular voyage to Wellington, lying across the Cook Strait on the North Island. Although there had been storm warnings for the area that evening, the Cook Strait is well-known for its rough seas, and there was nothing to suggest that this night's weather would be any dirtier than on any other night.

This night, however, was different. Cyclone Giselle was moving southwards towards Wellington, while from the southern Antarctic waters came another storm. These two storms, the one a warm, tropical storm, the other a cold Antarctic monster, collided head on directly over Wellington, creating winds of over 50 knots, and whipping up a huge sea. As the *Wahine* approached Wellington harbour a little after 5.30 am on the morning of 10 April, the storm was reaching its height. Rather than wait off the coast, however, and give himself sea-room in which to ride out the storm, the skipper of the *Wahine*, Captain Hector Robinson, decided that the best course of action would be to run for the shelter of the harbour. By this time his radar was no longer working, and visibility was down to almost zero.

A little over quarter of an hour later, the *Wahine* was abeam of Pencarrow Head, along the eastern side of the harbour, when she was struck by an enormous wave. At the same time the wind speed increased dramatically, churning up the sea and making the *Wahine* almost impossible to steer. Despite the best efforts of Captain Robinson and his crew, at around 6.30 am their ship was blown to starboard, and smashed onto the Barrett Reef around Pencarrow Head. She was holed below the waterline, and water began to pour through the rip in her side into the engine room, with predictable consequences.

As the engines failed, leaving the *Wahine* powerless, with no way of steering and grounded on the reef, her captain and crew were left little more than spectators, with their ship at the mercy of the wind and tide.

Around thirty minutes later, the waves lifted the stricken ship off the reef, and began carrying her further into the harbour. By dropping both

The Wahine *inter-island ferry was caught in a storm as she approached Wellington harbour and struck a reef*

anchors in mid-channel, Robinson was able to halt the drift of his vessel to a degree, but the huge waves continued to force the *Wahine* further into the harbour. Around 1 pm, as the *Wahine* was abeam the Steeple Rock Light, the tide began to turn, swinging the ship round to face the open ocean, and further increasing the already dangerous list to starboard.

Realising that the situation was now critical, at 1.20 pm Captain Robinson gave the order to abandon ship.

Despite the fact that only the starboard lifeboats could be launched, all the passengers and crew were taken off the now sinking ship, but the wind and waves wreaked a terrible toll, swamping or capsizing the *Wahine's* rubber rafts.

Many passengers were drowned, others swept onto the rocks of the harbour by the pounding surf; still others made it ashore only to die of exposure while waiting for medical attention to arrive. In all, some 51 people lost their lives that day.

A Court of Inquiry set up two months later found that although errors had been made, both aboard the *Wahine* and on shore, in particular the failure of those on shore to muster sufficient craft for a rescue, these errors had been made under conditions that were difficult and dangerous in the extreme, and as such, blame could be attached neither to Captain Robinson and his officers, nor the Wellington harbourmaster.

The *Wahine* was eventually demolished where she lay, in 6 fathoms of water, in Wellington Harbour; her foremast now stands in Wellington's Frank Kitts Park as a memorial to her dead.

9 Mysteries of the Deep

One of most enduring maritime mysteries is what happened to the captain and crew of the *Mary Celeste*, a hardy brigantine found floating unmanned in the middle of the Atlantic Ocean five hundred miles south of the Azores, apparently undamaged.

Originally a British vessel, she had been built in the shipyard at Spencer's Island near the head of the Bay of Fundy, and launched in 1861 under the name *Amazon*. From the beginning she seemed to be jinxed. Her first captain died within two days of registering her; her hull was damaged during her maiden voyage; she was damaged by both fire and collision. Following an accidental grounding at Cow Bay in Cape Breton in 1868, she was sold and began operating out of New York under an American flag. Her new master Captain Benjamin Briggs renamed her the *Mary Celeste*.

Briggs was an experienced mariner from a seafaring family. On 5 November 1872, he left New York's East River bound for Genoa with a cargo of crude alcohol. He was accompanied by his wife Sarah, his young daughter and a crew of seven.

The night before he left, he and his wife had dinner with Captain David Morehouse, an old friend who was bound for Gibraltar a few days later on the *Dei Gratia* with a cargo of petroleum. It was Morehouse who found the *Mary Celeste* floating in a calm sea 600 miles off Gibraltar on 4 December.

When Morehouse's men boarded her, they found the *Mary Celeste* silent except for the creaking of her timbers. Everything seemed to be in good order – though it appeared that the ship had recently been abandoned and in some haste. Breakfast lay half-eaten on the table; there was the clear imprint of a child's body on an unmade bed; an open bottle of cough mixture stood on a narrow shelf, its cork and a spoon lying beside it. The sea had been calm

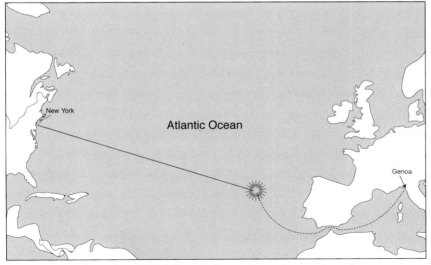

Location of the Mary Celeste *where she was found drifting and abandoned on 4 December 1872*

119

Clipper ship of the same type as the Mary Celeste. *Built for speed, these ships were exceptional sailers*

and not a drop was spilt. The crew's oilskins were still in the forecastle, along with a strong box and some women's jewellery.

The last entry in the log was dated 24 November and put her 170 miles west of Santa Maria Island in the Azores, 370 miles from her current position. That did not mean that the crew had gone missing that day. Captains don't make entries in the log every day. But, by coincidence, an unfinished letter written by the first mate to his wife, dated 25 November, talks of him having a nightmare where he was murdered at sea.

However, several things were missing – the ship's papers and navigation books, the sextant and the chronometer and, most significantly of all, the lifeboat. The eerie fate of the crew of the *Mary Celeste* was made famous by a story written by Sir Arthur Conan Doyle who mistakenly identified her as the *Marie Celeste* and deepened the mystery by saying that the lifeboat was still on board when she was found.

Morehouse towed the *Mary Celeste* to Gibraltar where he was immediately accused of piracy. It was suggested that he put three cutthroats on board to murder the crew and take the ship for salvage. But though sixty-six pages of testimony were taken, the attorney general could not make the charges stick. Morehouse was set free and claimed salvage. He got just one tenth of the value of the ship and her cargo. The *Mary Celeste* went back to sea and met her end scuttled on the Rochelois Reef off Haiti in 1884.

A great many theories have been put forward to explain the mystery of the *Mary Celeste*. The most likely is that she found herself in some unknown danger and everyone took to the boats. Although the captain plainly had the foresight to take the instruments he needed to navigate, they never made shore. No bodies were ever found, but the Atlantic Ocean is big and very, very deep.

But what caused them to abandon ship? It may have had something to do with the industrial alcohol in the cargo hold. It is a very volatile liquid and something may have caused Briggs to fear that it was going to explode. In a small boat, in November, it would not be difficult to lose sight of the mother ship, and a sudden squall could have sunk a ship's boat in open water in seconds.

The *Patriot* and Theodosia's Ghost

The schooner *Patriot* set sail from Georgetown, South Carolina, bound for New York on 30 December 1812. The passengers included twenty-nine-year-old Theodosia Burr Alston, whose husband John Alston, the governor of South Carolina, had seen her off. She was also the daughter of the former vice-president Aaron Burr, who she was on her way to visit.

When the *Patriot* was found floating off Nags Head on the Outer Banks in January 1813, there was no one on board. No one knows what happened to those on board. There had been a storm off Cape Hatteras at the time they were due there, but at least two former pirates made deathbed confessions, claiming they had plundered the ship and murdered the passengers and crew.

There is a story that Theodosia was washed ashore in a small boat after being set adrift by the pirates who had killed everyone else on board. She was taken in by a fisherman and his wife who cared for her until she was elderly. In 1869, she was ill and a doctor was called. He was told that he could take anything in the house he wanted in payment. He chose a portrait of a radiant young woman hanging on the wall. But Theodosia jumped from her sickbed and grabbed. It was her portrait, she said, and it was a present for her father in New York. It eventually found its way to the Burr family.

It is said that her ghost, dressed in white, can be seen walking on the crest of the waves off Huntington Beach, Nags Head. The locals believe that she was kidnapped by the pirates, but then lived as the common-law wife of one of them.

The *Carroll A. Deering*

Another unmanned schooner turned up off the Outer Banks in 1921. The *Carroll A. Deering* was on her way from Rio de Janeiro, heading back

The Carroll A. Deering, *pictured before her mysterious disappearance*

empty to Norfolk, Virginia, under the command of Captain Willis Wormell with a crew of eleven – five New Englanders and six Scandinavians.

The last port the ship had made was Bridgetown, Barbados, possibly to pick up a cargo of rum as Prohibition was in full swing. There, Wormell confided to a friend that he had no confidence in the crew.

On 31 January, she passed the Frying Pan Shoal lightship off Cape Fear. Six days later, after an extended nor'easter with 75-mile-an-hour winds had pounded the waters southwest of Hatteras, the five-masted schooner sailed past the Cape Lookout lightship. Someone aboard called out through a megaphone: 'We've lost both anchors and chains in the gale off Frying Pan Shoals – forward word to our owners.'

The lightship's engineer photographed the schooner. She seemed in good shape with her sails well set, though it was noted that her crew were hanging about on the deck in undisciplined fashion. Late the following afternoon, a northbound steamship sighted a five-masted schooner twenty-five miles southwest of Diamond Shoals lightship, apparently steering directly for Hatteras itself.

At 6.30 am on 31 January 1921, the *Deering* was spotted off Diamond Shoals by a lookout at the Cape Hatteras coastguard station. Lifeboats went out and arrived near her an hour later. It was too rough to board, but she appeared to be deserted. The ship's boat was missing and a ladder hung over the side.

A party from a coastguard cutter managed to get aboard four days later. By then she was in a pitiful state. In four days on the shoals her seams had opened and her hold was full of water. In the galley, there was a pot of coffee, a plate of spare ribs and some pea soup. Three ship's cats were found aboard. It was found that her steering had been deliberately sabotaged and the ship's maps were strewn around the bathroom. The FBI investigated the mystery but came up empty handed. A few weeks after she arrived on the shoals, the wreck of the *Carroll A. Deering* was dynamited as a hazard to shipping.

The Bermuda Triangle

One of the great mysteries of the sea is the Bermuda Triangle, said to be responsible for the disappearance of countless ships and their crews over the ages. To mariners this area of the Atlantic Ocean has always been a hazard. Known as the Sargasso Sea, it was first mentioned by Christopher Columbus. A clockwise current collects free-floating weed called sargassum, the presence of which in this instance erroneously suggests that land is near. Towards the centre, there is little current and, in the calm air, sailing ships were frequently becalmed. Early sailors had an unfounded fear of becoming entangled. Sitting on a motionless boat in the hot sun with little drinking water, it would have been easy to believe that the great raft of seaweed around you was inhabited by strange creatures.

In the nineteenth century there were reputed to have been mysterious wrecks and abandoned ships in the area. Advocates even claimed that the *Mary Celeste*, found far to the northeast, was a victim of the Bermuda Triangle. In February 1880, the British frigate *Atlanta* vanished en route from Bermuda to Portsmouth with 290 hands. Other ships reported a capsized vessel and the Atlantic was strewn with debris from gales that month.

Throughout the 1920s, 1930s and 1940s numerous losses across the north Atlantic and inside the Gulf of Mexico have been ascribed to the Bermuda Triangle. So far, though, no serious devotee has tried to blame the triangle for the loss of the *Titanic*.

The idea of a mysterious Bermuda Triangle developed much later and began with missing planes, rather than ships. At 2.10 pm on 5 December 1945, five US navy Avenger torpedo bombers took off from Fort Lauderdale Naval Air Station on a routine patrol. Flight 19 was to fly

160 miles due east out over the Atlantic Ocean, turn and head north for forty miles, then fly directly back to its Florida base. The patrol should have taken around two hours.

The weather was good. All the aircrews were experienced, and the planes were in good working order; each carried a full load of fuel and an inflatable life raft, and each man wore a Mae West life jacket.

At 3.45 pm, the patrol leader, Lieutenant Charles C. Taylor radioed base that he was out of sight of land and lost. The control tower told him to fly due west until he reached the coast. Taylor replied that his compass was not working.

For Taylor, Fort Lauderdale was a new posting and he was unfamiliar with the area. Although he was over the reefs and cays just north of the Bahamas – almost exactly on course – he thought he was over the Florida Keys. When he reported this to Lieutenant Robert F. Cox, a flight instructor from Fort Lauderdale, Cox told him to turn and fly north, keeping the sun on his left wing. Several of the other pilots were convinced that all they had to do to reach home was head west until they hit land. But military discipline meant they all stayed together and followed their commander north.

At 5.55 pm a radio fix was made on Flight 19, putting its position a hundred miles north of the Bahamas, over the Atlantic, fifty miles east of New Smyra, Florida. But the teletype was down so the control tower at Fort Lauderdale could not be informed.

Taylor now became convinced that he was in the Gulf of Mexico and turned east in the hope of reaching land. But in fact, this meant Flight 19 was heading further out to sea. It grew dark and the patrol was rapidly running out of fuel.

The control tower at Fort Lauderdale instructed

Flight 19 had 'vanished as completely as if they had flown to Mars'. The myth of the Bermuda Triangle was born

Taylor to switch to an emergency frequency that would be clear of interference. Taylor refused, fearing that he might lose contact with some of the other planes in the patrol in the switch-over.

At 6.10 pm, the radio fix was telephoned to the control tower. By that time, however, Flight 19 was out of radio range and could not be contacted. However, some of the radio conversation between the pilots was overheard. They were changing course yet again. Reception ceased at 7.04 pm. It was estimated that Flight 19 had enough fuel to stay in the air until 8 pm.

When the Air Sea Rescue Station at Banana River got the radio fix, three Martin Mariner flying boats were despatched. Rescue plane 49 called in its departure report just before 7.30 pm. It was due to call in again at 8.30 pm but nothing was heard. At 9.12 pm the duty officer heard that at 7.50 pm the crew of the SS *Gaines Milles* had seen an airborne explosion at approximately the position plane 49 would have been at that time. The ship's captain had said that the plane appeared to catch fire in the air, hit the water and explode. The crew saw an oil slick and debris. The crew of thirteen from plane 49 joined the fourteen missing men of Flight 19.

The following day an extensive search was made. No debris from Flight 19 was ever found. The oil slick and debris from the Martin Mariner had also disappeared.

When the story of Flight 19 is related, it is always emphasised that the weather was good and the visibility unlimited. It was – over Fort Lauderdale. Over the Bahamas, on the other hand, the weather was bad that night and the seas were rough. It was not a good night to ditch in the ocean and any remains of the planes would have quickly broken up and sunk. The story would remain alive due to a chance remark made by one officer at the board of enquiry. He said the planes of Flight 19 had 'vanished as completely as if they had flown to Mars'. The myth of the Bermuda Triangle was born.

A year to the day after the disappearance of Flight 19, the triangle began swallowing ships – or rather, their crews. The sloop *City Belle* en route from Nassau to the Turks Islands was found at sea deserted. However, there had been a storm that week and the *Nassau Guardian* reported that seven survivors had been picked up by an American lifeboat; although these reports have yet to be verified.

In March 1948, famous jockey Al Snider and two friends moored their rented cruiser off Sandy Key at the tip of Florida and rowed off in a skiff to go fishing. They were never seen again. But it was a dark and stormy night. A few days later, the battered skiff was found beached near the Everglades.

In September 1950, Associated Press put out an article linking the disappearance of the freighter *Sandra* with the loss of Flight 19 and these other 'mysterious' disappearances in the area. The article mistakenly said that the *Sandra* had gone missing in June. *Fate* magazine picked up on the story and pointed out that the weather in the area was calm throughout that month. The *Sandra* had actually gone missing in April during a hurricane.

In December 1954, *Southern Districts*, a freighter hauling sulphur, went down in the Straits of Florida with all hands. But she was generally considered unseaworthy and the sea was rough.

The yacht *Connemara IV* was found completely abandoned between Bermuda and the Bahamas on 29 September 1955. A hurricane had been through the area a week before.

And so it continued with report after report of missing aircraft and shipping, abandoned craft, missing fishermen and scuba divers. Lighthouse

There is little real evidence that ships and aircraft are more likely to go missing in the area of the 'vile vortices' than anywhere else

men vanished and people disappeared from beaches.

Nineteen-sixty-three was a particularly busy year. In February, the *Marine Sulphur Queen* went missing in the Gulf of Mexico. In July, the *Sno' Boy* and her forty occupants went down on a voyage out of Jamaica. Debris and a body were found. On 28 August, two USAF stratotankers disappeared. Debris was found and it was assumed that they had collided in mid-air.

Local newspaper reporters began ascribing crashes and disappearances to a mysterious 'Bermuda Triangle'. The southern corners of the triangle were supposed to be the tips of Florida and Puerto Rico; the northernmost Bermuda – or in some versions the Azores. Nevertheless, many of the incidents ascribed to the Bermuda Triangle occurred outside this area.

Professional mystery hunters began to look into the disappearances in the area. Captain McCains on a Deep Submergence Research Vessel claimed to have seen a sea-monster five thousand feet down in the area. There was talk of magnetic anomalies and that the triangle was the site of the lost city of Atlantis. A more scientific suggestion is that methane hydrate crystals at the bottom of the ocean sublimate, drastically lowering the buoyancy of the sea and the aerodynamic lift of the air.

The Bermuda Triangle is not the only area of the ocean where ships and planes disappear mysteriously. Between the coast of Japan and the island of Iwo Jima is the Devil's Sea. Nine ships were lost in that area between 1950 and 1955. However, the area is studded with reefs.

In 1968, Ivan T. Sanderson and the Society for the Investigation of the Unexplained identified twelve 'vile vortices' around the world. These are all on the latitudes 30 degrees north and 30

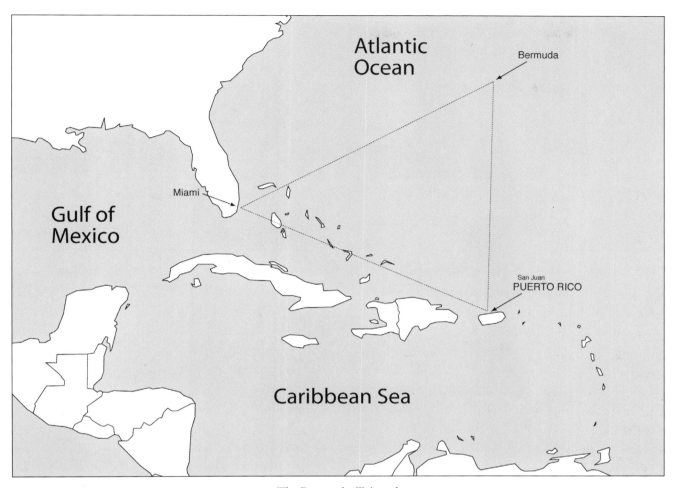

The Bermuda Triangle

degrees south of the equator and include the Bermuda Triangle, the Devil's Sea and Afghanistan, where a number of American military aircraft went missing during World War II. However, there is little real evidence that ships and aircraft are more likely to go missing in these areas than anywhere else.

Researcher Larry Kusche took a more rational approach. A reference librarian at Arizona State University, Kusche was intrigued by the number of requests he got for information on the Bermuda Triangle. So he contacted Lloyd's, the US coastguard, other government agencies and reviewed newspaper reports back as far as 1851.

The results of his research were published in *The Bermuda Triangle Mystery Solved.* In the book, he explains that there is no one theory that explains the disappearances in the Bermuda Triangle, just as there is no one theory that explains all the automobile accidents in Arizona. But if you look at the hard evidence in each individual case, you will find a plausible explanation for most of them. Many, of course, because the vicissitudes of the sea, will remain a mystery forever.

'The legend of the Bermuda Triangle is a manufactured mystery,' he said. 'It began because of careless research and was elaborated upon and perpetuated by writers who either purposely or unknowingly made use of misconceptions, faulty reasoning and sensationalism.'

10 Famous Wrecks

In the seventeenth century, Sweden was a great power in the Baltic region and wanted a navy to match. On the afternoon of Sunday 10 August 1628, the naval dockyard in Stockholm launched the *regalskeppet* – or royal ship – *Vasa*, which took its name from the Swedish royal house of that time. The massive ship was not only expected to keep the encroaching Habsburg Empire out of the Baltic, it was a symbol of royal power and national pride. One of the biggest ships in Europe at the time, she was 226 feet long, thirty-eight feet wide and displaced 1,210 tons. With a high forecastle and sterncastle, she had two gun decks with sixty-four guns in all, forty-eight of which were heavy 24-pounders.

A crowd of ten thousand watched from the shore as the *Vasa* fired two salutes from her guns, then set sail on her maiden voyage across the harbour to the naval base on the Stockholm archipelago. A sudden gust of wind hit the sails causing the ship to heel slightly. The sailing officer was just shouting orders to slacken the sails when they were hit by another gust. This time the gun ports dipped beneath the water line, and, as had happened to the *Mary Rose*, water poured in, flooding the lower decks. The *Vasa* rolled over on her port side and sank with all flags flying. Little more than half of her crew of 133 survived. It was a huge blow to national prestige, particularly as the country was at war with Poland at the time. Attempts were made to raise the *Vasa*:

within days an English salvager had managed to get her upright, but it proved impossible to lift her from the bottom. Salvage experts from all over Europe flocked to Stockholm to try their hand, with no success. Working from a primitive diving bell, the Swede Albrecht von Treileben managed to salvage her valuable cannon between 1663 and 1665. But the *Vasa* herself had to remain under the dark waters of the Baltic for another three hundred years before she was raised.

The *Vasa* had been lying at the bottom of Stockholm harbour for nearly three centuries when researcher Anders Franzén realised that in the cold waters of the Baltic it might still be in one piece. The Baltic is not salty enough for the teredo worm, which eats the hulls of wooden ships, to thrive: it is the only sea where the big men-of-war from the sixteenth and seventeenth century could be preserved.

He searched the archives to find her exact position, then he started exploring the seabed, first with a grapnel and a core-sampler which produced positive results. A diver was sent down; at a hundred feet he found a huge ship standing on her keel. It was too dark and muddy to see, but he could feel the ship's sides and there appeared to be no end to it.

There was nationwide interest in raising the *Vasa* and Sweden's Neptune Salvage Company was called in. They proposed digging six tunnels under

The Vasa *as she appears today in Stockholm's Vasa Museum*

She was gradually moved to shallow water where the damaged parts of her bow and stern were sealed. New gun ports were installed and the hundreds of holes left by iron bolts that had rusted away were plugged. Then she was floated on her own keel into a dry dock. Finally on 24 April 1961 she broke the surface – for the first time in 333 years.

Then the marine archaeologists got to work, both on the raised hull and the hole she had left on the seafloor. More than 25,000 finds were made. These included cannon balls, musket balls, clothes, plates, flasks, bowls, barrels, a backgammon set and fishing gear. And in the sail locker there were six spare sails that had not been set for her maiden voyage.

As no similar find had been made before, no one knew how to treat the wreck. However, a Swedish company called Domsjö had patented a preparation of polyethylene glycol, used for preserving fresh wood, which was found to work even better on waterlogged wood. A sprinkler system was installed and for the next seventeen years the *Vasa* was sprayed with polyethylene glycol until the timbers were saturated. More than five thousand new iron bolts were added to stabilise the hull. A conservation laboratory was built to preserve loose items and hundreds of pieces of wood underwent prolonged treatment in huge baths. These were then used to rebuild the damaged bow, sterncastle and rigging.

Conservators found themselves doing a huge jigsaw puzzle as no plans of the *Vasa* existed and there were no paintings or drawings of her. The

the hull. Steel cables would then be passed under her and attached to lifting pontoons. The Swedish navy provided the divers. Working blind, they had to blow the silt away with water jets. It was dangerous work as they had to crawl under the three-hundred-year-old wreck whose hull was filled with rock as ballast. Even if the whole thing did not come crashing down on top of them, it was all too easy to get stuck.

It took two years to get the cables in place. Once that was done, in August 1959, the water was pumped out of the lifting pontoons and the *Vasa* broke free of the silt.

seven hundred wooden sculptures that adorned the *Vasa* were cleaned and repainted – some were embossed with gold leaf. Finally, the spare sails were gently unfolded and washed, then dried with xylene and alcohol, and stuck to Fibreglass backing with a special glue.

The artefacts unearthed by archaeologists were displayed in a temporary museum from 1962 until June 1990, when a permanent museum was opened by King Carl Gustaf XVI to house both the ship and her contents.

A Tudor Rose

Armed with ninety-one heavy guns, the *Mary Rose* can boast of being the first modern battleship. Built in Portsmouth, she was launched in 1510 and policed the Channel for thirty-five years – a vital task as Calais still belonged to England. In 1512 she served as the flagship of the English fleet, under the Lord High Admiral Sir Edward Howard, at the Battle of Brest. According to contemporary accounts, the *Mary Rose* was a fine sailing ship. The fastest of the English vessels, she was dubbed 'the flower of the fleet' by Howard.

In 1536, she was completely rebuilt, uprating her from 600 to 700 tons. Although she already had a full complement of muzzle-loading bronze and breech-loading iron guns, the hull was strengthened with diagonal braces so that the main gun deck could carry more, heavier guns.

In 1544, Henry VIII seized Boulogne. In an effort to recover it, the French king sent his entire fleet of 200 ships, along with twenty-five galleys from the Mediterranean to bottle up the English fleet. On receiving news of their arrival off the Isle of Wight on 18 July 1545, Henry rushed to Portsmouth where, according to Sir William Monson, Henry dined on board the *Mary Rose* on 19 July 1545. That evening, he ordered the fleet out to meet the French off Spithead. He watched from the battlements of Southsea Castle as his flagship the *Mary Rose* led the English fleet out of

Portsmouth harbour. She quickly outran the rest of the fleet and, when she came under fire, she put about to fire a broadside and wait for support. As she turned, a sudden gust of wind caught her and she heeled over. Her new heavy deck guns were seen to break loose and crash into her leeward side, fatally unbalancing the ship. Her lower gun ports, which were just sixteen inches above the water line, had not been closed, and as they dipped beneath the water, the *Mary Rose* quickly filled and sank as Henry looked on in horror. On board were 185 soldiers, 200 seamen and thirty gunners, most of whom drowned trapped by the splinter netting rigged to protect them from flying splinters of wood during combat. Of the 415 souls aboard the *Mary Rose*, only thirty-five survived.

(A second *Mary Rose* was lost in Boston Harbour on 27 July 1640, one of the first warships to be lost in New England. Governor Winthorp of Massachusetts recorded in his journal that, at around dinnertime, she simply exploded. It is thought that a sailor had taken a candle into the hold which was packed with gunpowder. Only one man survived. He was picked up by a ferryboat, but could remember nothing of the explosion or his rescue. Despite the explosion, the ship was salvaged.)

The search for the wreck of the *Mary Rose* was begun in 1965 by diver Alexander McKee, but it was Professor Harold Edgerton of the Massachusetts Institute of Technology who located her using the latest acoustic equipment. She was completely buried in mud, making diving surveys unproductive until a gale at spring tide removed three feet of sediment to reveal eight timbers. Diving on the wreck then proved productive and by 1979 it was clear that four of her decks were preserved and her starboard side, at least, was intact.

In 1979, the Mary Rose Trust was formed with the aim of preserving and possibly raising her. Further examination revealed that the hull was sound as it was held together with wooden treenails: the internal structure, however, was only held in place by severely corroded ironwork and silt.

Steel cables were attached to the hull and it was lifted into a cradle, which was then lifted onto a barge. The *Mary Rose* emerged from the waters of the Solent in 1985. The immediate problem was how to conserve her. She had been preserved in the oxygen-free environment under the mud, but in the air she would quickly crumble. The hull was taken to a disused dry dock, which was given a roof. The wreck was constantly sprayed with cold fresh water, and the air was kept at four degrees, with a relative humidity of 95 per cent.

A model of the Mary Rose, *the flagship of King Henry VIII's fleet, which sank in the Solent in July 1545. The remains of the Tudor warship have recently been brought to the surface and are now on display in Portsmouth.*

The conservation programme had actually started three years before she was raised. A detailed examination of the timbers showed that the wood inside was sound, but the outer layers had been attacked by bacteria and rotted before the wreck had been covered. But it was these outer layers that needed conserving, as they showed the marks left by the carpenters and revealed the method of construction.

A new phase of conservation started in 1994, when the temperature was raised to 18°C and the *Mary Rose* was sprayed with two types of polyethylene glycol. This was to continue for at least twenty years, after which time the hull would be allowed to dry out. More than 22,000 artefacts were brought up with the *Mary Rose*. These included navigation equipment, spare rigging, guns, gun carriages, powder flasks, cannon balls, canister shot comprising sharp pieces of flint, 138 yew bows and 3,500 arrows. Human remains revealed evidence of social status and occupational stress, while seeds in the remains of clothing told experts more about sixteenth-century agriculture. Many of these finds are now on show in the Mary Rose Museum in the Royal Naval Base in Portsmouth.

A flute, gaming board and pieces, and a leather-bound diary salvaged from the wreck of the Mary Rose

The *Lusitania*

On 22 April 1915, the Imperial German Embassy in Washington, D.C., had the following warning printed in the New York newspapers:

—— **NOTICE** ——

Travellers intending to embark on the Atlantic voyage are reminded that a state of war exists between Germany and her allies and Great Britain and her allies; that the zone of war includes the waters adjacent to the British Isles; that, in accordance with formal notice given by the Imperial German government, vessels flying the flag of Great Britain, or of any of her allies, are liable to destruction in those waters and that any travellers sailing in the war zone on ships of Great Britain or her allies do so at their own risk.

The notice appeared in the New York World next to an advertisement for the Cunard liner *Lusitania*. That same day the 32,000-ton *Lusitania* steamed out of New York harbour with 1,959 passengers and crew on board. She was the only large liner still plying between Britain and the United States. The others had been requisitioned for military service. Indeed some of them had even been involved in the fighting. The pride of the German passenger fleet, *Kaiser Wilhelm der Grosse*, had been converted into an auxiliary cruiser. While refuelling at sea, she was attacked by the converted Cunard liner *Campania* and damaged so badly that it took a year to repair her.

The German notice was no idle threat. German U-boats were prowling the waters of the North Atlantic. On 5 May, *U-20* under the command of 32-year-old Lieutenant-Commander Walther Schwieger sank the schooner *Earl of Latham* off the Old Head of Kinsale on the south coast of Ireland. The following day he torpedoed the liner *Candidate* in St George's Channel, sinking another civilian vessel, the *Centurion*, soon after.

As no one was killed in these sinkings, there was no doubt that there was a U-boat at work in the area. But there was little the British could do about it. Coastal defences were minimal and the Royal Navy was overstretched. HMS *Juno* was sent to patrol the area, but she was old and slow and next to useless against a fast-moving submarine.

On 7 May, as the *Lusitania* approached southern Ireland, the admiralty broadcast a radio message warning British shipping to stay away from the shore, avoid headlands where U-boats were known to lurk, and travel at full speed. However, with passenger revenues down, Cunard had shut down one of the *Lusitania's* four boiler rooms, leaving six of her twenty-five boilers idle, to save on coal. This cut her top speed from twenty-six to twenty-one knots. There was patchy fog off the Irish coast that day and Captain William Turner ordered the *Lusitania* to slow. He did not even zigzag, claiming later that he thought zigzagging was a tactic you adopted after you saw a U-boat. However, he did order the liner's watertight doors to be closed.

Uncertain of his position, Turner steered towards the shore to look for familiar landmarks. He spotted the Old Head of Kinsale, which told him he was near Cork harbour. It also meant that he was in *U-20's* prime hunting ground. To fix his position more accurately, Turner decided to take a four-point bearing. To do this, he had to keep the ship on a straight course for forty minutes.

Schwieger had spotted the *Lusitania* at around 1 pm and dived to about thirty feet. He headed straight for the liner whose steady course and slow speed made her a sitting target. At 2.09 pm he fired a torpedo. A lookout on the *Lusitania* cried: 'Torpedoes coming on the starboard side.'

The torpedo hit the *Lusitania* just aft of bridge. After the torpedo blew up, holing her, a larger explosion followed. This might have been one of the boilers exploding or coal dust in the

The New York Times.

VOL. LXIV...NO. 20,923.   NEW YORK, SATURDAY, MAY 8, 1915.—TWENTY-FOUR PAGES.   ONE CENT In Greater New York, Jersey City and Newark.

LUSITANIA SUNK BY A SUBMARINE, PROBABLY 1,000 DEAD;
TWICE TORPEDOED OFF IRISH COAST; SINKS IN 15 MINUTES;
AMERICANS ABOARD INCLUDED VANDERBILT AND FROHMAN
WASHINGTON BELIEVES THAT A GRAVE CRISIS IS AT HAN

SHOCKS THE PRESIDENT

Washington Deeply Stirred by Disaster and Fears a Crisis.

BULLETINS AT WHITE HOUSE

Wilson Reads Them Closely, but Is Silent on the Nation's Course.

HINTS OF CONGRESS CALL

Loss of Lusitania Recalls Firm Tone of Our First Warning to Germany.

CAPITAL FULL OF RUMORS

Reports That Liner Was to be Sunk Were Heard Before Actual News Came.

Special to The New York Times.
WASHINGTON, May 7.—Never since that April day, three years ago, when word came that the Titanic had gone down, has Washington been so stirred as it is tonight over the sinking of the Lusitania. The early reports told that there had been no loss of life, but the relief that those advices conveyed gave way to the greatest concern late this evening when it became known that there had been many deaths. Although they are profoundly reticent, officials realize that this

The Lost Cunard Steamship Lusitania
X Where the First Torpedo Struck.   XX Where the Second Torpedo Struck.

Cunard Office Here Besieged for News; | **Roosevelt Calls It Piracy;** | **Meagre List of Saved** | **Loss of the Lusitania Fills London**

SOME DEAD TAKEN

Several Hundred ors at Queens and Kinsal

STEWARD TELLS OF D

One Torpedo Crashes Doomed Liner's Bow, Into the Engine R

SHIP LISTS OVER

Makes It Impossible Many Boats, So H Must Have Gone B

ATTACKED IN BRO

Passengers at Luncheon Had Been Given by Ge fore the Ship Left Ne

LONDON, Saturda —The Cunard liner which sailed out of N last Saturday with 1 aboard, lies at the b the ocean off the Iris She was sunk by a submarine, which sen pedoes crashed into h 2:30 o'clock yesterd noon while the p seemingly confident great, swift vessel c

The New York Times *records the torpedoing of the* Lusitania *off the coast of Ireland by a German submarine*

half-empty coal bunkers igniting. It has also been suggested that the *Lusitania* was carrying 173 tons of rifle ammunition and shells and these too might have exploded. The bridge was torn apart and caught fire. Within seconds the *Lusitania* began to list to starboard and started sinking quickly by the bow.

Schwieger noticed confusion on the decks of the *Lusitania*. As people were already in the water, he decided not to put another shot into the stricken liner and left the scene before the Royal Navy arrived. The *Lusitania* took just eighteen minutes to sink.

The *Juno* and other ships were soon on the scene to pick up survivors. There were just 761 of

them. Of the 129 children on board ninety-four were lost and only four of the thirty-five infants survived.

One of the survivors was Captain Turner. He had been washed clear when the ship sank. His testimony to the court of enquiry was confusing and contradictory, leading some conspiracy theorists to suggest that the British deliberately sank the *Lusitania* to hasten America's entry into the war. Although he admitted that he was too far inshore, he also said that he thought submarines were far more likely to prowl in open waters further out. Nevertheless the court of enquiry exonerated him and praised him as a 'skilled and experienced' master. The court of enquiry found that 'the loss of the said ship and lives was due to damage caused to the said ship by torpedoes fired by a submarine of German nationality whereby the ship sank. In the opinion of the court the act was done not merely with the intention of sinking the ship, but also with the intention of destroying the lives of the people on board.'

The British used the sinking of the *Lusitania* to depict the Germans as monsters who happily murdered women and children. The Germans countered this propaganda by saying that they considered the *Lusitania* to be an auxiliary cruiser in the Royal Navy, like her sister ships the *Campania* and the *Mauretania*, and that she was carrying munitions for the British war effort – which was probably true – so she was a legitimate target. But the dead included 128 Americans. This turned American public opinion against Germany. Although America did not abandon its neutrality for another two years, when it came into World War I on the side of the British, it cited Germany's indiscriminate use of submarine warfare as a reason.

Captain Turner went on to take command of the troop carrier *Ivernia*, torpedoed off the Greek coast in 1917 with the loss of 150 soldiers and crew. After the war, he became commodore of the Cunard Line. Schwieger was killed in action in 1917 on board *U-38*.

Lessons were learnt from the sinking of the *Lusitania*. The British liner *Arabic* practised lifeboat drill and zigzagged as she approached the southern coast of Ireland. Even so, she was hit by a torpedo just fifty miles from where the *Lusitania* had gone down three months before. Her wireless was put of action, so she could not call for help. Listing to starboard, she sank in just nine minutes. In that time, only six lifeboats got away, but 379 of the 423 people on board survived. They were picked up an hour after the sinking. Some of the casualties were American and this increased anti-

The torpedo hit the *Lusitania* just aft of the bridge: the ship took just eighteen minutes to sink

German sentiment in the US. Again Germany defended its policy of sinking unarmed passenger ships without warning, saying that the captain of *U-24*, Lieutenant-Commander Schneider, had mistaken the Arabic's zigzagging for an attempt to ram his submarine and had torpedoed her in self-defence.

The *Lusitania* lies nine miles off the coast of southern Ireland in 295 feet of water. She was located in 1935, using early echo sounding equipment. Later that year divers went down to investigate the wreck, and the Royal Navy conducted some salvage work on her in 1946. Then in the early 1960s, an American diver named John Light bought the wreck from the British government. He began a series of dives to try and discover the cause of the second explosion, which was the real cause of her rapid sinking, but he was unable to come to any firm conclusion.

In 1982 a consortium headed by Oceaneering International spent a month working on the wreck. They raised the bow anchor, three of the ship's four bronze propellers, portholes, one of the ship's whistles, a docking telegraph, and plates and utensils. They also found several hundred military fuses, proving that she had been carrying munitions. Oceaneering claims that it was the detonation of these munitions that caused the ship's demise, but has declined to publish its evidence.

In 1993, Dr Robert Ballard, the marine scientist who had located the wrecks of the *Titanic* and the *Bismarck*, tried to solve the mystery. Diving on the wreck, he found that she was in a bad state of decay, and the hull was in two pieces. It was thought that the bow had come away when the ship hit the bottom. It pointed up at forty-five degrees and the name on her side was still visible. The *Lusitania*, festooned with fishing nets, was lying on her starboard side, hiding the area where the torpedo struck. The superstructure and the deck had collapsed and the hull had sagged under its own weight, leaving the ship roughly half its original width.

Ballard and his team took thousands of photographs and sixty hours of video, but they were unable to come up with a 'smoking gun'.

'We found nothing to suggest the ship had been sabotaged,' he said. 'Nor was there evidence of an explosion in the ship's magazine, which is presumably where contraband munitions, if any, would have been stowed. The other strong possibility, a boiler explosion, seems highly unlikely since none was reported by any of the survivors from the three boiler rooms in operation.'

However, they did find numerous lumps of coal strewn across the sea floor, which must have been scattered as she sank. Ballard believes that the torpedo probably ripped open one of the starboard coal bunkers, which would have been nearly empty near the end of the transatlantic run. This impact would have kicked up a cloud of coal dust. Coal dust mixed with air is an explosive combination and this could have been the cause of the second explosion that sent her so rapidly to the bottom.

The real cause will probably never be known. In 1994, the ownership of the *Lusitania* became the subject of a court battle. The following year, the US District Court in Norfolk, Virginia, awarded ownership and salvage rights to a businessman from New Mexico who claimed to have bought them from John Light. However, this only applied to the fabric of the ship and its appurtenances, not to the cargo or the personal effects of the passengers and crew. Then the Irish government stepped in (the *Lusitania* lies in Irish territorial waters). The Minister of Arts and Culture slapped an underwater heritage order on the wreck and banned any further diving on it without government permission which, so far, has not been forthcoming.

The Most Famous Wreck of All

When the *Titanic* set off on her maiden voyage from Southampton to New York on 10 April 1912, she was the largest and most luxurious ship afloat. Cigar holders had been provided in her washrooms and more first-class cabins had been built on B deck, in a space that Ismay had noticed passengers rarely used aboard the *Olympic*. Her four funnels were big enough to have two trains driven through each of them and her propellers were the size of windmills.

Within her nine decks there would be accommodation for 3,547 people – 905 in first class, 564 in second class and 1,134 in third class. The other 944 on board were crew. The best suites, which were oak-panelled, cost $4,350 one way – over $80,000 in today's money. The 882.5-foot *Titanic* was one of the first ships to have a swimming pool, and the gymnasium had the latest exercise machines from Germany. The grand staircase was lit by a chandelier and a darkroom developed passengers' photographs during the voyage.

Although the designers never said that the *Titanic* was unsinkable, many believed that she was. She had a double hull made of iron, the outer skin of which was an inch thick. Inside there were sixteen watertight compartments four of which could be flooded without endangering the ship's buoyancy. Captain Smith certainly had no doubts about her. He had long thought the age of the shipwreck was over. He had said of the *Adriatic*, an earlier behemoth in the White Star Line: 'I cannot imagine any condition which would cause a ship to founder. I cannot conceive of any vital disaster happening to this vessel. Modern shipbuilding has gone beyond that.'

The *Titanic* was thought so safe that the Board of Trade did not revise the number of lifeboats she should carry to match the increased number on board. The lifeboats could handle only half of the passengers and crew if she was fully booked. There were only sixteen wooden lifeboats and four collapsible life rafts – provision for just 1,178 out of 2,224 people on board. This worried no one. It was thought that, even if she did get into trouble, she would sink slowly like the *Republic*, leaving plenty of time for other ships to come to her assistance, so the boats would only be needed to ferry people back and forth.

The transatlantic elite were on board the *Titanic* for her maiden voyage. These included John Jacob Astor – reputedly the richest man in the world – with his young wife, and Ida and Isidor Straus, the owners of Macy's, then the world's largest department store. The owner Bruce Ismay was also on board, along with campaigning journalist W.T. Stead who was on his way to a peace conference in New York. The voyage was also due to be Captain Smith's last: he intended to retire having sailed with the White Star Line for thirty-eight years.

He took the *Titanic* on a northerly route in the hopes of making a faster passage. It was April and although the ship had received warnings that there were icebergs in the area, Captain Smith discounted them, remarking that he had never known of ice so far south at that time of the season. He was wrong. At 11.40 pm the lookout, Fred Fleet, in the crow's nest saw a huge iceberg dead ahead. He sounded the alarm and the engines were thrown into reverse. But it was too late. The ship might even have been saved if she had sailed straight into it. But Captain Smith had

Surviving passengers from the Titanic *are taken on board the* Carpathia *on the morning of 15 April 1912*

lingered over a second cigar after dinner that evening and the inexperienced officers on the bridge threw the helm hard to port and the iceberg struck the *Titanic* a glancing blow on the starboard bow, covering the foredeck with ice and tearing a huge gap in her side.

At first the liner appeared so lightly damaged that most of the passengers and crew refused to believe that she was going to sink. But below the water line, the iceberg had ruptured the hull and six of her watertight compartments began to fill. It was then that a fault in the design became apparent. The walls of the watertight compartments did not go all the way to the deck above and, as one filled, the water spilt over into the next. Twenty minutes after the collision, five compartments were full and it was clear that the *Titanic* was going down.

At 12.30 am Captain Smith gave the order to man the lifeboats. There was so little concern among the passengers at first that some lifeboats left less than half full: Sir Cosmo and Lady Duff Gordon set off in a lifeboat with only twelve on board, when it was designed to carry forty. As the situation developed, the rule of 'women and children first' was applied, but husbands and fathers still expected only a short separation from their loved ones. By 2 am all the lifeboats had left. Over 1,500 people were still on board and their perilous position was becoming clear. As the deck began to slope precipitously, alarm spread: there were reports of a shot being fired to quell disorder. Some people leapt into the icy waters far below, while others huddled together on the stern. A number of third-class passengers were trapped below decks by locked gates and an officious steward.

The *Titanic* took two-and-a-half hours to sink. Throughout that time the lights of another ship,

Twenty minutes after the collision, five compartments were full of water, and it was clear that the *Titanic* was going down

seemingly oblivious to the distress rockets fired from the stricken liner, could be seen on the horizon. By 2.17 am the water had flooded all the *Titanic's* forward compartments, raising the stern high out of the water. The hull snapped between the third and fourth funnel and the great ship disappeared beneath the black Atlantic waters.

The ship seen on the horizon was the liner *Californian*. Although she was less than twenty miles away, and could have been on the scene in plenty of time to save the wrecked passengers and crew of the *Titanic*, tragically her wireless operator was not on duty that night, and the *Titanic's* desperate appeals for help went unheard. The *Carpathia* did hear the *Titanic's* distress calls, though, and steamed full ahead to the rescue, arriving just eighty minutes after the huge ship had gone down. But few could survive more than a few minutes in the freezing water. One who did was a baker who had spent the evening fortifying himself with alcohol while helping others into the lifeboats. Once they were all away, he stepped off the stern and bobbed about drunkenly in the water for several hours before being rescued, apparently warmed by the alcohol. Jack Thayer, heir to a Philadelphia fortune, also escaped with his life. He leaped into the water when it was still around twelve feet below the rail and swam away as fast as he could. He narrowly missed being crushed by one of the funnels and was nearly sucked under as the ship finally went down, but he bumped into an upturned life raft and was hauled aboard.

In all, 705 people were rescued, 1,519 lost their lives. Among the dead was John Jacob Astor who, at the last minute, had asked to accompany his pregnant wife on the lifeboat. When his request was refused, he quietly walked away. When his body was found there was $2,000 in his pocket.

While the lifeboats were being loaded with women, Ida Straus handed her necklace to her maid, Ellen Bird and stated that she was staying with her husband. 'We have lived together these many years. Where you go, I go.' Friends tried to convince her to change her mind, but she would not budge from her husband's side. Her husband was equally impervious to persuasion, stating firmly, 'I will not go before the other men.' Mrs. Straus put her arm around her husband and the two of them walked away from the boats.

W.T. Stead retired to the first-class smoking room, where he was last seen engrossed in his book. Captain Smith went down with his ship.

The sinking of the *Titanic* spawned a series of lawsuits. This began in the American courts, but the Supreme Court ruled in 1914 that all the US claimants had to band together and bring a class action suit. But the *Titanic's* only assets in the US were $91,805.54 in unpaid passenger and freight fees, thirteen lifeboats and their equipment. Meanwhile in the English courts, the relatives of four passengers trapped in steerage sued the White Star Line, claiming that their family members had been killed by the negligence of the company's employees. White Star denied this and pointed to a waiver that excluded the company from liability, which was printed on the back of the ticket. The English courts found that this waiver was invalid. They also found that there had been negligence and awarded the plaintiffs £100 each in compensation. So the US claimants began taking action in the English courts. Their claims totalled $16 million. On 28 July 1916, White Star made an out-of-court settlement for $664,000 in damages for loss of life, personal injury and loss of personal effects, provided all other suits on both sides of the Atlantic were dropped. Eventually it was White Star's insurer, the Liverpool and London Steamship Protection and Indemnity Association Ltd, that paid up.

The wreck of the *Titanic* was discovered by Dr Robert Ballard four hundred miles off the Newfoundland coast in 13,100 feet of water in September 1985. It was surveyed in the summer of 1986 by a joint US-French team using remote control photographic equipment. The hull was found to be in two pieces. The stern, badly damaged and looking like it had suffered an internal explosion, was found sitting several hundred yards away from the largely intact bow. The keel had sliced deeply into the mud, holding it upright. The crow's nest was still attached to the foremast, but was gone when the wreck was surveyed again in 1998, and the foremast itself was by then buckled and twisted.

A salvage effort in 1987 found a missing propeller and more than three thousand items have since been raised from the wreck. In 1991, submersibles took IMAX equipment down and brought back pictures of extraordinary clarity. Then in 1995, in preparation for making the movie *Titanic*, film director James Cameron sent robotic equipment to investigate the interior. The robot eye glided down the main staircase and into the sitting room of a first-class suite on the starboard. It found the remains of a chair and a fireplace with its brass firebox still intact. In the reception room outside the first-class dining room on deck D the camera found wood panelling and the ship's distinctive octagonal ceiling fixture was still in place. One of the main entry doors for the first-class passengers was still on its hinges and its decorative iron grillwork was visible.

An ultrasound examination of the area of the bow hit by the iceberg revealed, not a huge gash 250 feet long as expected, but a series of six small tears opening into the first six compartments. The iceberg, it seems, had not torn through the metal, but had popped the rivets allowing the plates to separate, sending the world's first 'unsinkable' liner to her watery grave.

The Titanic *(above left)* begins her long journey to the ocean floor; *(above)* the final resting place of the world's most famous ship, two and a half miles under the Atlantic

11 Survivors

On the morning of 4 June 1629, the Dutch ship *Batavia* ran aground on the then uncharted Morning Reef, two miles from Beacon Island in the Abrolhos archipelago, some forty miles off the coast of Western Australia. She was on her way from Texel in the Netherlands to Batavia – modern-day Jakarta – to buy spices. That April the *Batavia* had become separated from the rest of her convoy by a storm off the Cape of Good Hope and there was talk of mutiny on board. The ship's drunken and violent skipper Ariaen Jacobsz and an undermerchant named Jeronimus Cornelius aimed to throw the company's senior man Francisco Pelsaert overboard, seize the ship and take to a life of piracy.

In the run-up to the planned mutiny, the conspirators made a night-time attack on a young lady named Lucretia van der Meylen, who Pelsaert had befriended. However, Lucretia recognised one of her assailants, Jan Evertz, by his voice. Pelsaert intended to hang Evertz when they reached the 'Unknown Land' which we now know as Australia: the mutineers agreed that this punishment was to be the signal for the mutiny to begin. But before that happened the ship ran aground.

Jacobsz, Pelsaert and forty-six of the crew took most of the food and water and landed on a small island. The other 268 passengers and crew landed on a larger island that became known as Batavia's Graveyard. Without water, many died within the first few weeks. Refreshed by a little rain, Jacobsz and Pelsaert buried their differences and set off for Batavia in the ship's boat, leaving a note for the other survivors on what, after that, became known as Traitors' Island.

Cornelius took charge, and gradually revealed himself as a highly dangerous psychopath. With his band of mutineers, he instigated a reign of terror, murdering anyone who opposed him. Lucretia was forced to become his mistress on pain of death. Dressed in fine clothing rescued from his ship's stores, Cornelius and his men experimented with new ways of meting out misery and death to the other survivors. Those who tried to escape to other islands were ruthlessly hunted down and killed, if they had not already perished from thirst and starvation.

The only effective threat to Cornelius's power was a number of soldiers who had been on board. Cornelius sent them to look for water on the other islands under the command of a soldier named Wiebbe Hayes, expecting them to fail and, hopefully, perish in the attempt. Not only did they find water, they found numerous seabirds and their eggs and they sent smoke signals to tell the others they had been successful.

Some stragglers reached Hayes on 'High Island' and told him what Cornelius was up to. As Hayes prepared to defend High Island, Cornelius administered a loyalty oath to his men and got ready to attack. But the mutineers were no match for the soldiers and two assaults were repelled. Cornelius then tried to negotiate peace, but during the talks he tried to bribe some of the soldiers to join him. Hayes seized Cornelius. Three of the leading mutineers were killed and one escaped.

It took thirty-three days for Jacobsz and Pelsaert to reach Batavia. When they arrived, the boatswain was arrested and executed, on Pelsaert's indictment, while Jacobsz was charged with negligence. The governor-general sent Pelsaert and the yacht Sardam to rescue the survivors. It took them sixty-three days to find the wreck site. They arrived on 16 September, just in time to witness the last battle between Hayes and the mutineers.

Hayes and some of his men escaped the fray to warn their rescuers. Pelsaert rounded up the mutineers and tried them for the murder of 125 of their fellow survivors. Some had to be tortured into making confessions; others freely confessed. Cornelius and the ringleaders were hanged. Two others were marooned on the coast of Western Australian. The rest were taken back to Batavia. On the way, they were flogged, keelhauled and dropped from the yardarm. When they arrived, they were executed.

Out of 316 people aboard the *Batavia*, only 116 survived. Pelsaert died in the following year, but he left a journal which led searchers back to the wreck in 1963. In 1972, the Dutch government transferred rights to the wreck to the Australian government, who passed the Historic Shipwrecks Act in 1976 to protect it, and today it is a popular dive site.

A bulldog named King was hero of the hour when the British troopship *Harpooner* bound from Quebec to England ran onto a reef in fog off Newfoundland at 9 pm on 20 November 1816. On board were 385 men, women and children. A gale was blowing and the masts were cut away. The ship's boat was smashed to pieces in the collision.

Some of the crew managed to get ashore in the smaller stern boat, but could not return to pick up the others because of the surf. The ship now lay on her beam ends and the waves washed over her.

Stuck on the reef some three hundred yards from shore, the ship was now in danger of breaking apart. The men on the shore climbed a rock and indicated that those on the stricken vessel should send a line over. The captain tried to float the log line ashore, but when the men on the shore failed to find the line in the darkness, he came up with an alternative plan. The end of theline was tied around King's waist, and he was lowered into the slack water in the ship's lee. Battling his way through the raging sea, King eventually reached the rocky shore, where he was washed off five times before he eventually managed to climb out of the water. With the line in place the crew managed to set up a boatswain's chair which carried the passengers to safety one by one. The first woman ashore was pregnant and gave birth two hours later.

However, the *Harpooner* broke up before everyone was ashore. The last person off was 70-year-old Lieutenant Mylrea, one of the oldest subalterns in the British army. He jumped in the water and floated ashore. Two hundred and eight people, including Captain Bryan, died. One hundred and seventy-seven people, and one dog, survived.

A famous rescue at Bamburgh, Northumbria took place on 7 September, 1838. The previous night a violent storm had sunk the SS *Forfarshire* at the Big Harcar rocks, three-quarters of a mile from the Longstone lighthouse, manned by William Darling and his family. Out of the sixty passengers and crew on board, nine escaped in a lifeboat and another nine survived by clinging to rocks.

At dawn the following morning, William's daughter Grace spotted the survivors on the rock through a telescope and together with her father, rowed out across a heavy sea in the lighthouse coble to save the survivors. At the first attempt they took off five, and while Grace remained at the

Grace Darling and her father set off on their mission of mercy to rescue the stranded crew of the SS Forfarshire

lighthouse to tend three of the survivors, her father and the other two returned to collect the others. The nine survivors, four crewmen and five passengers, remained on Longstone lighthouse for three days until returning to the mainland when the storm had subsided.

When they finally reached the mainland, Grace became a heroine. The newspapers happily exaggerated her story and, for the Victorians, she became the very model of female courage. She died of pneumonia just four years later and was buried in Bamburgh churchyard. A memorial, built to be visible to passing ships, now stands over Grace Darling's grave, the money raised by public subscription, Queen Victoria herself contributing £20. St Aidan's Church now boasts a stained glass window depicting the rescue and there is a Grace Darling Museum in Bamburgh, under the care of the Royal National Lifeboat Institute.

The Birkenhead Drill

Another act of selfless heroism was to seize the public imagination in 1852. On the evening of 25 February, the British troopship *Birkenhead*, a 1,900-ton iron paddle steamer, left Simon's Town, South Africa, on the last leg of her voyage from Ireland to the Eastern Cape. On board were 680 souls. Over two hundred were soldiers of the Sixth Foot, the rest crew and paying passengers, among them twenty women and a number of children.

On the way, she had to pass the rocks and shoals of Danger Point. The captain Robert Salmond had plotted a course that missed the point by three miles. But either because of strong currents or a compass error, the *Birkenhead* drove directly onto the rocks. There were only eight lifeboats – only enough to carry two hundred of the 680 aboard. Three got away carrying the women and children.

Meanwhile Salmond ordered the engines full astern to drag the ship off the rocks. In doing so, however, he only succeeded in making damage worse. Below, several stokers drowned and it became plain that the *Birkenhead* was sinking. Colonel Alexander Seton, a thirty-seven-year-old Scot commanding the Sixth Foot, drew his men up on deck as the rigging crashed around them. He gave those who could swim permission to jump over the side and attempt to save their own lives. But as they rushed for the rails, he stopped them.

'Stand fast, I beg you,' he said. 'Do not rush the boats carrying the women and children. You will swamp them.'

Only three men disobeyed his orders and dived overboard. The rest held their ranks until, minutes later, the *Birkenhead* broke her back and disappeared under the waves. Captain Salmond, Seton and more than four hundred drowned. But among the 193 survivors were all the women and children on board. Since then, the order 'women and children first' has been known as the '*Birkenhead* drill', celebrated in the Rudyard Kipling's poem 'Soldier an' Sailor Too':

> To take your chance in the thick of a rush,
> with firing all about,
> Is nothing so bad when you've cover to 'and,
> an' leave an' likin' to shout;
> But to stand an' be still to the Birken'ead drill
> is a damn tough bullet to chew,
> An' they done it, the Jollies –
> 'Er Majesty's Jollies –
> soldier an' sailor too!

The Birkenhead Drill: soldiers, sailors and Marines calmly await their fate as the women and children are saved first

Index

Picture Credits

Illustrations on pp 6, 23, 34-5, 138-9 by Roger Hutchins

Photographs
AKG: 60
BBC: 107
Bridgeman: 13
Corbis: 130
Fotopress: 118
History Collection, Nova Scotia Museum, Halifax, Canada: 31
Hulton Getty: 4, 7, 8, 11, 44, 64, 67, 70, 80, 95, 99, 101, 115, 132, 135, 142, 143
John Liddiard/liddiard.demon.co.uk: 39
Leigh Bishop/Deep Image.Com: 47

Mary Evans Picture Library: 9, 42
Mike Boring: 61
National Maritime Museum: 57, 92, 112
Rex: 41, 75, 87, 88, 116, 127
Science Photo Library: 103
Topham: 129
United States Library of Congress: 110
United States Naval Historical Foundation: 19, 20, 21, 22, 23 28, 36, 37, 76, 77, 83, 84, 85, 105, 106